THE SCOTTISH OFFICE

RURAL SCOTLAND

People, Prosperity and Partnership

The Government's Policies for the Rural
Communities of Scotland

Presented by the Secretary of State for Scotland
by Command of Her Majesty
December 1995

EDINBURGH: HMSO

Cm. 3041   £22.50 net

ISBN 0 10 130412 9

FOREWORD

*Rt Hon Michael Forsyth MP,
Secretary of State for Scotland*

Rural Scotland has one of the most dramatic landscapes in Europe; although we largely take it for granted, we are living on one of the finest natural film sets in the world. Yet this romantic terrain is also the working environment for a wide variety of people who combine an important contribution to the economy with stewardship of our natural heritage. I am, therefore, pleased to present the first Scottish White Paper on rural policy. In it we set out, for the first time in one document, our policies for rural communities and the ways in which they are put into practice in the working landscapes of Scotland. We began in 1992 with *Rural Framework*. Now, I feel it right to offer the people of our rural communities a real voice in the decisions which affect the ways in which they live, to present them with a means by which even the most remote or isolated communities can seek to realise their own aspirations.

*Lord James Douglas-Hamilton
MA LLB MP, Minister of State*

*George Kynoch MP, Minister for
Industry and Local Government*

The *Scottish Rural Partnership* is a flexible approach to the empowerment of rural communities, working with the new councils and the main agencies whose task is to deliver services affecting rural life. It is intended to enable local action. So we will offer, through the National Partnership and the Fund, access to expertise and to experienced community agents who will assist communities to realise their own plans. The role of Government, and its agencies, is to provide the framework for those ambitions to be realised.

As well as the *Scottish Rural Partnership* system, we announce a number of important developments, such as the increased support for the village shop. We promise a wide range of advice and guidance to enable better services to be delivered and rural communities to take advantage of opportunities as they arise.

*The Earl of Lindsay, Minister for
Agriculture, Forestry and the
Environment*

These proposals have been brought together against the background of continuing close contact with a wide range of rural interests at all levels. I am grateful to all the organisations which have worked in partnership within

*Raymond S Robertson MP,
Minister for Education, Housing
and Fisheries*

the Rural Focus Group. We have been encouraged by the useful comments we have received from the consultations we undertook this year, both directly and with invaluable help from Rural Forum. This White Paper is the outcome of listening to what people want and we shall continue to listen and act accordingly.

My Ministerial colleagues in The Scottish Office each have responsibilities which support different aspects of the integrated policy outlined in this document. We will continue to work with the many organisations, within and outwith Government, which have already contributed so much.

I believe that we are making good progress towards achieving our aims; but there is much more to do. The proposals in this White Paper offer the best way for us all to work in partnership to achieve prosperity for the people of rural Scotland.

The Rt Hon Michael Forsyth MP
Secretary of State for Scotland

December 1995

CONTENTS

FOUNDING ON
FRAMEWORK

1   Rural Scotland is home to almost one third of the Scottish people who live in a wide variety of communities. We each know what kind of community we live in, and it is usually self evident when that is rural or urban. Each way of life has its own characteristics, advantages and opportunities. Each has its own set of challenges, requiring approaches and actions tailored to different situations.

2   At the same time, the people of Scotland are close-knit and rural and urban communities have many links. Those living in towns have close affinities with the countryside, which often begins not far from their homes; and the rural dweller is proud of the national institutions which the cities of Scotland offer. Their common characteristics in needs for jobs and services far outweigh their differences and we pursue policies based on the same fundamental principles in all parts of Scotland.

3   Government in Scotland, at all levels, is distinctively Scottish. Scottish policies have been developed here in Scotland, building on traditions, such as the broad base to education; institutions like the separate legal system; and our particular circumstances, such as the vast extent and outstanding quality of our natural and built heritage. Governments' first aim has been to ensure, as we said in *"Scotland in the Union - A Partnership for Good"*[1], that Scotland's identity as a nation is enhanced. Throughout history, rural Scotland has contributed enormously, perhaps disproportionately so, to our national and cultural heritage, and it is of the utmost importance that we maintain and build on our achievements.

4   The last comprehensive view of the needs of rural areas was almost certainly as long ago as the Scott Report of 1942 on *"Land Utilisation in Rural Areas"*[2]. That offered thoughts to stem the *"drift from the land"* and the future of agriculture. The flow of population has been reversed, albeit that the incomers are often people with different backgrounds from those who have been born and brought up in those areas. Some of the issues, such as agriculture, remain highly topical although today the context is different, that of the Common Agricultural Policy.

5   In the late eighties, there were demands for a new approach to rural communities. The House of Lords Select Committee on the European Communities, in its Report on *"The Future of Rural Society"*[3], recommended that a 'bottom-up' approach be complemented by regional and national strategic guidance. In 1990 Borders Regional Council, supported by the Convention of Scottish Local Authorities, mounted a major conference on *"Rural Development: Future Strategies"* which led to calls

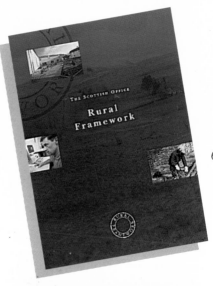

The *Rural Framework* Themes

Community Involvement: The strength of the rural community lies in its people; it is vital that they be involved in decisions about their future.

Diversity: once a common feature of rural communities needs to be re-established and pursued.

Quality: Rural Communities deserve high quality services and need to produce high quality products.

Local Added Value: Value added locally to the resources supplied by rural Scotland will retain the profits locally and benefit its communities.

Effective Service Delivery: By working together, local authorities, public agencies, the private and voluntary sectors will best deliver their services in ways which most benefit their customers.

Networks and Communications: Rural Scotland can use its remoteness to advantage through the development of networks and communications.

Europe: Rural Scotland has a place in Europe which it can use to its own and others benefit.

Sustainability: By pursuing our actions today in a sustainable manner we will protect ourselves and safeguard our descendants.

for a national strategy to guide all those working for the improvement of life in rural communities. But having a strategy sometimes seemed to be a goal in itself without much thought being given to its content. The Government took action in 1989 to bring a co-ordinated approach to its own work within The Scottish Office, with a single Minister charged to maintain an overview of rural issues.

Rural Framework

6   However, it was evident that despite the abundant goodwill on all sides to work together towards the goal of an integrated approach, there were obstacles. A major stumbling block was the lack of a common language with which apparently unrelated sectors could talk to each other and work towards a common end. In 1992, the Government published *"Rural Framework"*[4]. This made a number of important statements about the Government's approach to rural communities. Perhaps the most important of these was:

"the realisation that tackling rural issues in a sectoral manner does not work"

7   This is not to reject the contribution that can be made by organisations established on a sectoral basis. For many it is the only sensible way to work: Scottish Homes' first priority must be housing, that of the Enterprise network must be economic prosperity. But in pursuing their main objectives each offers something to the other. A common set of overall aims could help each organisation to produce more from the resources available to it.

8   The Government proposed eight themes in *Rural Framework* which are fundamental to improvement of life in rural communities. They were not offered as axioms of rural policy nor as a central prescription for the way forward. Government was keen not to hinder the progress of organisations which were well-advanced in the plans and programmes. Several organisations needed time to develop their strategies following recent re-organisation or establishment - Scottish Homes, Highlands & Islands Enterprise, Scottish Enterprise and the network of local enterprise companies, Scottish Natural Heritage, the Scottish Agricultural College.

9   *Rural Framework* built on a thought put forward in the 1942 Scott Report which said that:

"Much that we propose requires good will rather than money".

By 1992 substantial resources were already being deployed through local authorities and Government agencies but *Rural Framework* was about cooperation, and working towards more effective output through a co-ordinated approach. *Rural Framework* was well received and its eight themes have indeed proved to be an effective way of bringing together disparate interests. But the importance of the themes lay not in precisely what they said but in the fact that people were willing to use them to develop innovatory ideas.

Rural Focus

10   *Rural Framework* provided a new foundation for action and, later in 1992, the Government decided to give greater practical effect to its ideas. The Government established the Rural Focus Group which brought together The

Scottish Office and the main Government agencies, the Convention of Scottish Local Authorities, and the private and voluntary sectors, represented by Rural Forum.

11 The Group was asked, as the basis for its work, to take forward the ideas contained in *Rural Framework*. It has met regularly since 1992 working on:

- discussion of key issues affecting the future of rural Scotland, involving a wide range of interests. Outcomes include sponsoring of a major conference on *"Incentives to Rural Enterprise"* in Inverness in May 1994 which looked at the opportunities for rural Scotland under Objectives 1 and 5b of the EC Structural Funds;

- encouragement of research into important rural issues jointly funded by the bodies represented on the Group. Topics covered include rural child care in the Highlands and Islands funded by The Scottish Office and Highlands & Islands Enterprise, and rural transport options funded by The Scottish Office and COSLA;

- promotion of improved information about the range of financial and other assistance available in rural Scotland. The Group has overseen a project leading to the recommendation that an information booklet, similar to that produced by Tayside Regional Council, should be produced for other parts of rural Scotland. Rural Forum was commissioned to prepare a national template for this initiative and is working with local authorities to prepare local editions for publication when the new councils take up their responsibilities in April 1996;

- identification and encouragement of innovatory approaches to rural development. Examples include working with the Laggan Community Association on a feasibility study of proposals for development based on community-led tourism and woodland management; and evaluation of the potential of a new model for rural development pioneered by the Wise Group in Ross and Cromarty based on local training, job creation and environmental improvement.

12 Much has been achieved. The setting up of the Rural Focus Group has encouraged each individual agency to see its work in relation to that of others, and has demonstrated the value of a partnership approach. The Government believe it is now right to move on to a new stage in development by setting out, for the first time, the overall aims of rural Scotland which all bodies should have in mind.

Consultation

13 Our review of rural policy has addressed a number of areas. In particular, we have been keen to understand what people with an interest in rural communities feel about what has been done and what ideas they might have for making the most of new opportunities. The consultation has taken three forms:

- a progress report from the Rural Focus Group

The Rural Focus Group was established to:

"provide a forum for the examination of issues affecting rural areas and to promote collaboration among central Government, its agencies, local government and the private and voluntary sector for the improvement of the quality of life in rural areas".

Rural Focus Members:

- Central Scotland Countryside Trust
- Convention of Scottish Local Authorities
- Forestry Commission
- Highlands and Islands Enterprise
- Rural Forum
- Scottish Agricultural College
- Scottish Enterprise
- Scottish Homes
- Scottish Natural Heritage
- Scottish Tourist Board
- The Scottish Office, in the chair

Progress since Framework

The Government has supported the work of the Rural Focus Group since its formation in 1992 and welcomes the Group's independent views offered in *"Rural Framework: A Progress Report"* which is published simultaneously with this document. The report describes many of the practical steps which rural organisations have been taking since the *Rural Framework* concept was launched.

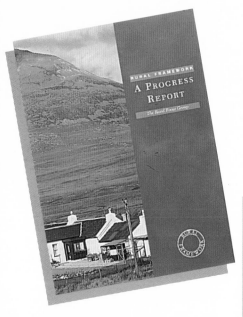

- a series of conferences and workshops undertaken for The Scottish Office by Rural Forum;

- an invitation to all those who expressed an interest in Rural Framework to offer comments.

The Rural Focus Group

14 The Rural Focus Group has examined how far each of the Rural Framework themes has been put into practice in the last three years and, in its report[5], demonstrates the progress that has been made in improving the quality of life and prospects for rural areas.

The Rural Focus View of Progress on the *Rural Framework* themes:

- **community involvement** has increased. Better coordination and targeting of activity would help to ensure all areas and sectors are covered and community agents would be a useful way to encourage more communities to get involved in local issues;

- the **diversity** of rural businesses has improved. Continued support through training and advice is essential in order to encourage businesses to be flexible in the long term;

- the **quality** of Scottish produce continues to be high and opportunities still exist to market products on the basis of high environmental and animal welfare standards. Coordination of quality standards is important, to avoid confusing consumers.

- some progress has been made in **adding local value** to products, but opportunities remain particularly in the food processing and forestry sector. Advice is needed on the establishment of small businesses and to help them develop small-scale production systems that meet modern standards of hygiene and product safety;

- in **effective service delivery** there are good examples of joint funding, collaborative research and giving of information and advice. The potential for delivery of joint services, through sharing of premises, staff and information networks has yet to be fully realised and there is considerable scope for further progress here;

- advances in technology have gone some way to overcome the problems of remoteness in rural communities through improvements to **networks and communications**. There have been transport improvements too, but concerns remain about the increasing reliance of rural communities on private car ownership and maintaining public transport;

- **Europe** has offered both funding opportunities and a broader range of information and expertise to rural Scotland, as well as greater access to European markets for rural businesses. There is also greater control in terms of meeting environmental and health regulations and the UK Governments recognition of this factor in negotiations with the European Commission is welcomed;

- there is much happening in rural Scotland to promote the idea and practice of **sustainable** development and the progress made is welcome and encouraging.

Reporting the Consultations

Rural Forum organised the consultation exercise across Scotland. Its report on the consultation and the many helpful and interesting things said in that process is published simultaneously with this document in *"The White Paper Consultation: the Rural Forum Report"*.

15 Action has been taken by a wide range of bodies and while many of the projects mentioned are supported by Rural Focus members, many are run by other organisations. The report arrives at two general conclusions:

● good progress has been made in many areas and much of it achieved through partnership, particularly at a local level. This should be built upon, more local partnerships encouraged and experience from existing partnerships made available to others;

● Rural Focus itself has demonstrated partnership at national level and through research, seminars and discussion has made a useful contribution to rural policy coordination. A more systematic programme of research, monitoring and evaluation is now needed, which would identify examples of good practice and disseminate this information to all those involved in the development of rural Scotland.

The Public Conferences, Workshops and Comments

16 The Government regard the public consultations, from conferences, workshops and written submissions as an important exercise, building on a similar process which followed the publication of *Rural Framework*. It has been important not just to hear the ideas and wishes of individuals and organisations but also to enable these thoughts to be shared. This enables others to understand the concerns of specific interests and cooperate in taking advantage of opportunities. The process of exchange and discussion is vital to the improvement of life in rural Scotland.

Main Conclusions of the Public Consultation Exercise

The consultation exercise which underpins and informs the White Paper had two elements. Over 900 organisations and individuals were asked to offer thoughts on future rural policy against the background of *Rural Framework*. Rural Forum was commissioned to hold a series of discussion workshops and seminars throughout Scotland. From these sources some common thoughts emerged:-

● there was a need for an **integrated strategy** for economic and social activity in rural areas.

● a **Rural Aid Fund** would help promote the development of rural small business, training and development enterprises.

● the growth of **teleworking** has much to offer for the future prosperity of rural Scotland.

● there might be benefits to **crofting**, if new land could be made available for the creation of new crofts.

● **good practice** in local service arrangements should be identified, monitored and disseminated particularly where it involved innovative approaches.

● **diversification of farm income**, including expansion into tourist, sporting and craft activities should be encouraged.

● the **rural transport infrastructure** should be protected and developed.

● the **Common Agricultural Policy** should move away from subsidies on production and towards the provision of integrated support for rural economies.

● encouragement should be given to the development of **rural housing associations** to combat the drift of rural populations in some areas to urban centres.

● links between **health, employment and the ageing of rural populations** should be explored in a much more systematic fashion, in order to develop strategies for an overall improvement in these areas.

● **animateurs** should be available to stimulate and nurture small business enterprise in rural areas.

● the provision of **child care facilities** in rural areas would release the skills and experience of working women.

The Corrom Trust

- The Corrom Trust provides, through its Scottish Rural Programme, co-ordinated funding and professional advice to support regeneration in rural Scotland. This programme brings together Rural Forum, COSLA, British Telecom and Scottish Homes to establish local partnerships with Scottish rural communities. The Trust has been funded by its primary sponsor, the Tudor Trust, the AJAHMA Trust and the British Telecom Community Programme.

- The aim of the Corrom Trust is to empower local people to shape the future of their community on the basis that successful regeneration depends on local involvement. It uses well tested methods for public participation and places particular importance on involving young people. The overall aim is to mobilise resources in the community, increase co-ordination between local organisations and focus attention on an achievable and strategic programme of action.

Continuing the Effort

17 While *Rural Framework* was important in opening a new era of cooperation between all rural interests, there has been much other work done, in research and support for individual initiatives. Very many people are working hard for rural communities, not least through the voluntary sector. Highlands & Islands Enterprise has found that in its area alone there are over 3,000 voluntary organisations, equivalent to one for every 100 persons in the area. That pattern is repeated across Scotland. We have found that engaging with this huge resource of people, keen to take action themselves, is highly effective and productive.

18 Major players in enabling the voluntary sector to be heard are organisations such as Scottish Wildlife and Countryside Link; the National Farmers Union, Scotland; the Scottish Landowners' Federation; Rural Forum and the network of community councils and Councils of Voluntary Service. Not every demand made through this wide web can be met but it is vital that the two-way traffic between the centre and the community is maintained.

The Scottish Office Reorganisation

In common with other Government departments, in 1995 The Scottish Office reviewed its organisational and senior management structure. In the course of this exercise, the Permanent Secretary and the Review Team consulted major organisations, including those active in rural affairs, with which The Scottish Office deals in order to hear their views about how effectively the Office dealt with their interests.

From October 1995, a reorganised structure brings together responsibility for education and industry; and agriculture, fisheries and environmental affairs.

These changes bring the opportunity for closer, more effective and integrated working between those responsible for these matters with the aim of delivering real benefits to those whom The Scottish Office serves.

19 In later chapters we:

- examine what needs to be done based on research commissioned by many different organisations;

- make clear how the available effort can be harnessed for the good of rural communities;

- outline the steps we intend to take to enable communities to take command of action to benefit their people.

RURAL LIFE

20 In Scotland, rural policy is about the livelihoods of rural communities, the countryside and the lives of those who live in rural Scotland. While many of them live far from even quite small towns, the influence of the urban population is something which the rural dweller cannot ignore. In contrast, the town person can easily pursue an urban life without giving the countryside or its people a thought. Rural Scotland is sometimes seen by those living in our towns and cities merely as a convenient source of scenery, postcards and recreation, its management confused by the assumption that our countryside is part-museum, part theme park. The vital life blood which sustains our rural communities and through them our countryside and landscape, is a good deal more complex. The rural heartland survives through productivity, diversity and tradition; it thrives on the goods and services it can provide for the wider community, from food, fish and timber to tourism, culture and sports.

21 Presented in this way, it would be easy to regard the rural dweller as the poor relation. In truth, the similarities between life in the town and the country far outweigh the differences. The basic tenets of policy apply equally well to all, differing only in the precise terms of application. In order to develop policies which are of real benefit to rural communities, we need a common perception of rural life and an appreciation of the inter-relationship of policies. This was one of the underlying objectives of *Rural Framework*. The process begun by *Rural Framework* has been followed through with a series of documents intended to assist the development of rural policies. These have provided information, explanations of policy or guidance aimed at a wide audience. The first was *"Scottish Rural Life: A Socio-Economic Profile of Rural Scotland"*[5] which offered a picture of the way in which life is lived in Scotland's rural communities.

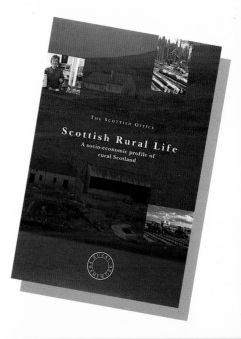

THE PATTERN OF RURAL LIFE

22 In the first part of this chapter, drawing on *"Scottish Rural Life"*[6] and research conducted by The Scottish Office and others, we attempt to describe the distinctive pattern of rural life in Scotland. This overview of rural life is drawn from research commissioned by The Scottish Office and by others, such as the Convention of Scottish Local Authorities and Rural Forum. Later we set out the policies and initiatives which impact on the social aspects of Scottish rural communities, economic issues and our policies to improve the competitiveness of rural Scotland.

The Rural Population of Scotland

23 Most people know when they are in a rural area. For some purposes, however, it is useful to have a definition and we have so far used one (often called the Randall definition) which defines as *rural* those local authority

Scottish Rural Life 1995

A new edition of Scottish Rural Life will be published soon, incorporating information drawn from the 1991 Census.

districts which have a population density of less than 100 persons per sq. km. Such districts account for 90% of Scotland's land and are home to just less than a third of its population. However, there is as much variation in the distribution and characteristics of the rural population as there is in its landscape and land uses. Population density varies widely from 2 persons to each square kilometre in Sutherland to 96 in North East Fife. In contrast, the population density in the new council areas of Edinburgh and Glasgow exceeds 1000 persons per sq. km.

24 While most rural Scottish people live within villages or other small settlements, fewer than 10% live in housing scattered in the countryside. One in twenty of the Scottish population lives in settlements whose population lies between 500 and 2,000. But even here there is wide variation. For example, in Skye and Lochalsh, two-thirds of the population live in settlements of fewer than 500 people whereas in Kyle and Carrick the equivalent figure is one-tenth. Between 1981 and 1991, there was a trend in some districts towards people concentrating in slightly larger villages rather than spreading more widely across the countryside.

25 Scotland contains some of the remotest parts of the United Kingdom and Europe. In *"Scottish Rural Life"* we published maps showing how long it took to reach a major service centre of 30,000 people or more. These showed that some one third of the population of rural Scotland live beyond a one hour drive and 11% have to drive more than two hours to reach such a centre.

Island Life

One of the features which makes Scotland so different to other countries in Europe is the number of its islands. There are over 500 islands in the three main archipelagos of Shetland. Orkney and the Western Isles, of which some 350 are populated. Their history is an integral part of that of Scotland and each has its own special magic, whether the sandy machair of the Uists, the continuing battle between land and sea in Shetland or the rolling land of Orkney. But they have many things in common with mainland rural Scotland, like remoteness and the way in which their lives have been built around agriculture and fishing. Since 1974 they have had a unitary form of local government, providing the full range of services to populations as small as 30,000 and each has its own health board.

We are committed to enabling the people of the Scottish islands to enjoy the same opportunities and levels of service as the rest of Scotland so far as that is practical.

Portnahaven, Islay

The way in which the population is changing

26 In 1942 the Scott Report was concerned about the movement of people to the city. After declining in the early years of the century, in the 1960s many rural districts experienced a period of rapid population growth. Between 1971 and 1981 the rural population increased by 8% and this continued, more slowly, through to 1991. Much of the rise in population in the 1970's and 1980's was associated with the growth in the oil

industry in the north and north-east of Scotland. Districts in the north east experienced the largest increases in population, some experiencing growth of over 20%. Whilst most of this increase can be attributed to in-migration, in these districts there was a significant increase in population because of more births than deaths. Other areas saw a population fall, such as Shetland, the Western Isles, Cumnock and Doon Valley and Caithness as people moved away and the population aged. The proportion of people aged over 65 compared to those under 14, has also increased in most rural districts. These broad trends look set to continue into the early years of the next century.

27   People moving into rural areas often compensate for the changes in the local population. In recent years all rural districts have experienced a net in-flow of population, although the presence of large towns in some of them may mean that this is more of an urban effect than one relating directly to rural areas. Employment opportunities are a key factor although in some parts of rural Scotland the scenic attractiveness of an area is the draw rather than the strength of the local economy. Rural Scotland has a higher than average proportion of in-migrants who are retired and these come mostly from elsewhere in Scotland. People coming from outside Scotland tend to take up residence in areas neighbouring the border and in Orkney and Shetland.

The Quality of Rural Life

28   For many people rural communities offer a high quality of life. But, for some, life is more difficult with some households being described as *deprived* if they are affected by its head being unemployed or permanently sick; having a low-earning occupation; overcrowding; household being large or having a single parent, or are all elderly. A multiply-deprived household is defined as being affected by two or more of these factors. Across Scotland as a whole 9.6% of households were classified as multiply-deprived according to 1991 Census indicators. A more detailed analysis of deprivation by settlement size reveals that in rural districts, those living in settlements under 1,000 population or outwith settlements were least likely to be deprived.

29   The nature and pattern of deprivation differs substantially between urban and rural areas. Although rural areas experience generally lower levels of unemployment, there is more dependence on low-paid or seasonal work. A report prepared for Rural Forum and the Convention of Scottish Local Authorities found that two thirds of heads of household in four rural areas had incomes of less than £200 per week, and low incomes were particularly common amongst older people and the unemployed. Uptake of state benefits was lower than expected given the level of incomes.

30   It is important, however, to recognise that rural dwellers themselves often do not consider themselves to be disadvantaged although they recognise that in some cases they have poorer access to services or affordable housing. For many, the other, perhaps intangible, benefits of rural life compensate for the lack of urban-style facilities. This has important implications for service providers and Government in seeking to meet the needs and wishes of rural communities.

Action on Deprivation

Local authorities are tackling rural deprivation and disadvantage, mainly by trying to meet specific needs such as service provision or transport. For example, Strathclyde Regional Council has established a Rural Challenge to provide funding for innovative and cost effective ways of addressing the problems of rural deprivation, improving service delivery in rural areas and disseminating good ideas and practice to other rural areas.

Rural Lifestyles

31   Two recent studies provide a fuller picture of life in rural areas. *"Rural Scotland Today: The best of both worlds?"*[6] and *"Living in Rural Scotland"* both explore various facets of rural life. The latter, a Scottish Office study, begins a comprehensive survey of life in four rural communities, against which it will be possible to monitor future change and the impact of policy.

Alex Hewitson, shepherd

Perceptions of living in rural Scotland

People like living in rural Scotland (recent research showed that 95% of people were satisfied with their rural community). They said:

● The main advantages of rural life related to the surrounding environment; peace and quiet and living in pleasant surroundings with friendly neighbours.

● The main disadvantages to living in a rural area were the lack of transport and shopping facilities though these were mentioned only by a minority.

● Rural settlements in more remote areas were most concerned about service provision.

● The need to retain young people in rural areas raised concerns about affordable housing and local employment opportunities.

● The difficulties caused for young local people competing in the local housing market was one of the perceived negative impacts of the influx of affluent commuters or retirement migrants to rural areas.

● Incoming households were thought to bring benefits such as children who would help to sustain local schools. Such households often have higher incomes and make a significant contribution to the local economy.

● There had been changes in the time that they had known the area but more thought that the area had improved rather than deteriorated and expected that this would continue.

Service Provision

32   *Rural Framework* highlighted the need for more effective service delivery. Against the trend towards centralisation of services, there is a role for more

imaginative ways of service delivery, for example sharing premises and mobile services. As part of the continuing work following from *Rural Framework*, The Scottish Office has commissioned a survey of rural services including education, childcare, health and social services, shops, post offices, meeting places and transport. Preliminary conclusions from the report, which will be published later in the year, are:

- **the vast majority of settlements have at least one food shop;**

- **most settlements have at least one non-food shop, such as a newsagent or gift shop;**

- **tourism has an important effect on shopping; one-third of settlements with a population less than 500 have a gift shop and 40% had a cafe or restaurant;**

- **child care facilities are confined to playgroups or mother and toddler groups but are available in 88% of communities. Only 30% have a local authority nursery and 12% a private establishment;**

- **play areas for children are available in the majority of settlements;**

- **village halls exist in three-quarters of all rural settlements and 80% have use of the village school.**

"Living in Rural Scotland"

Early in 1996, The Scottish Office will publish the report it commissioned on rural services.

Post bus, Highlands

Local Authority Action on Services

- *Annandale and Eskdale* has established a scheme to pool leisure and recreation equipment for loan to rural communities and another to provide free transport to and from rural areas to allow young people to participate in leisure programmes operated throughout the District. A similar scheme operates in East Lothian.

- In *Fife Region*, local service offices have been established in certain rural communities to promote community involvement in service delivery. Several post offices in more remote communities provide information about regional council services.

- *Highland Regional Council* established a Community Development Projects Initiative to assist community-based projects such as rural swimming pools, rural post offices and heritage centres. With the benefit of European funding, the Council has also developed a system for public information and service provision to rural areas, based on public multi-media computer terminals which enables public services which are routinely available in urban centres to be made available cost effectively to the most rural areas.

- Several local authorities run small business and rural shop assistance schemes and operate mobile libraries.

Education

33   Rural people feel that the quality of schooling in their areas is superior to that found in large towns and cities. Often the provision of care and education for children in rural areas also requires more planning because of the issues of transport availability, fewer premises and the more scattered population. Schools in rural areas can provide a focus for other social and cultural activities in the community. Although many young rural people feel there is much to be gained from spending time in urban areas, the lack of employment opportunities often means that they leave the community having obtained qualifications even if they wish to stay at home.

Westerton Primary School, Aberdeen

Change in Small Schools

Small schools form a substantial proportion of all Scottish schools, especially in the primary sector in rural areas. At times of rapid change in both curriculum and school management these schools may face particular problems in coping with the pressures of innovation.

The Scottish Office is to fund new research on "The Management of Change, including Devolved School Management, in Small Primary Schools".

The project will identify and examine the effectiveness of strategies adopted in small schools in response to recent innovations in Scottish education, including devolved school management in order to ensure the effective delivery of teaching and learning in such schools, so vital to community life in rural areas.

Video Conferencing In Argyll And Bute Primary Schools

● Primary schools in Argyll and Bute tend to be remote and small, the majority having fewer than 3 teachers. Strathclyde Education Authority is encouraging primary schools to group together in "co-operatives" to help staff development and to provide better support for head teachers.

● Within these co-operatives, schools have been provided with additional computers, CD-ROM and e-mail and a comprehensive staff development programme undertaken. After a pilot study, the BT VC8000 video conferencing system is being installed in 40 schools with help from BT and Olivetti in providing equipment and by giving free installation and initial line use.

● Computers in different schools can be linked together and a picture of distant pupils is available on each computer screen either full size for discussions or retained in a corner while the main part of the screen is being used for joint working between the schools. These electronic links allow pupils to see and talk to others of their own age in other schools, to learn together and to co-operate in joint projects. The system develops the IT skills of pupils and their ability to access and use information, an important factor when the potential for distant and home working is considered. Schools can share specialist teachers, in Gaelic and art and design for example, and staff development is improved through the sharing of experience and increased mutual support.

Rural Childcare

34 Recent research on childcare in rural areas noted that in the Highlands and Islands full day care in a nursery or creche was available to less then 3% of children under 5. Compared with the urban situation, rural children may have less access to full day-care, nursery education and out-of-school care. Access to registered childminders is more limited. Many economically active women in the Highlands and Islands Enterprise area make use of informal childcare provided by their spouse, other relatives or unregistered carers. Playgroups are a main source of care activity for most pre-school age children in rural areas.

Under-Fives Rural Initiative

April 1995 saw the completion of this pilot project which was intended to develop good practice in good quality day care in rural areas. Just over £0.5 million was made available to support the appointment of tutors to work alongside carers and playgroup leaders to assist those working in groups to increase the level of learning for the children attending. The results show that rural tutors can offer a valuable way to enhance the quality of these services.

Transport and Accessibility

35 Reflecting national trends, car ownership rates have been increasing steadily in rural areas in recent years. Changes in public transport provision over this period as well as changing work and shopping patterns and the centralisation of services and facilities have meant that private transport has become increasingly important to rural dwellers. Car ownership levels are higher in rural Scotland (69%) than in Scotland as a whole (57%). In contrast a, little over half of households in urban areas have use of a car.

36 The increase in car ownership and the convenience of having access to private transport in part explains the diminished demand for public transport. Transport needs in rural areas are likely to be very localised and small-scale and as a result different mechanisms of transport provision need to be considered. Where transport difficulties are experienced these will mainly apply to specific groups in the population such as young people, women who are at home during the day, and older people.

Key Points on Scottish Rural Life

In this overview of some of the main social and population trends affecting rural communities some key issues have emerged:

● The remoteness and diversity of Scotland's rural communities has implications for the planning and delivery of services.

● Rural communities are diverse.

● Rural Scotland is a popular place to live, as witnessed by the population growth, largely accounted for by in-migration to rural areas.

● Rural areas offer a wide range of benefits and migrants are attracted for a number of reasons, mainly related to employment and the general appeal of the area.

● In-migration has brought benefits where young families have moved into communities and sustained the local school, in other cases there is concern about the impact of affluent migrants on the local housing market.

● Housing and employment in the local area needs to be available for young people.

● Rural communities do not suffer from deprivation to the same extent as urban dwellers, but pockets of disadvantage exist. Local authorities and others have been active in attempting to tackle the problems faced by rural dwellers. Change is an inevitable component of rural life, whether through population movement or changes in employment. Thus the key challenge for rural policy is to develop approaches which are sensitive to the diversity of rural circumstances and changing circumstances faced by rural dwellers.

● Service delivery affects particularly the more remote communities.

Access to information and advice

● The Scottish Office will publish the results of research on how access to information and advice might be improved. It will recommend that local bodies agree a common approach to providing information in a way that meets local needs, which might include: well-publicised helplines; freephone or local call rate facilities; local contact points; and greater shared use of existing premises.

● A key recommendation was that Tayside Regional Council's booklet on rural grants, which was sponsored by the Scottish Agricultural College, should be extended to cover the whole of rural Scotland. This is now being taken forward by Rural Forum in conjunction with the relevant local councils, with assistance from The Scottish Office.

● Citizens Advice Scotland has received funding from *Scottish Power* and *British Telecom* to provide a national telephone advice facility which will be available at local call rates and will therefore be of particular benefit to people living in rural areas.

Rural Crime

Crime is an issue of increased concern to people who live and work in rural areas. We are committed to tackling crime in rural communities and in 1996 intend to mount a study to assess crime in rural areas and its impact on local people. Particular attention will be given to innovative ways of tackling local crime, especially drug and alcohol-related crime, that committed by young people and by people who live outwith rural areas.

Ullapool, Ross and Cromarty

SUPPORT TO THE COMMUNITY

37 In the second part of this chapter we look at some of the policies which meet the challenges set.

The Scottish Office Programme of Expenditure

38 Support for local government in Scotland represents the largest call on all funds available to the Secretary of State for Scotland. Allocations to councils are calculated on the basis of need with account being taken of features such as remoteness and sparsity of population which are particularly relevant to rural areas.

Collection of Commercial Waste

The arrangements adopted by local authorities for setting and administering charges for the collection of commercial waste have been a matter of concern to many small businesses in rural areas. We intend to identify examples of good practice in dealing with the particular problems of commercial waste collection in small towns and villages. This will be published as guidance for the new local councils.

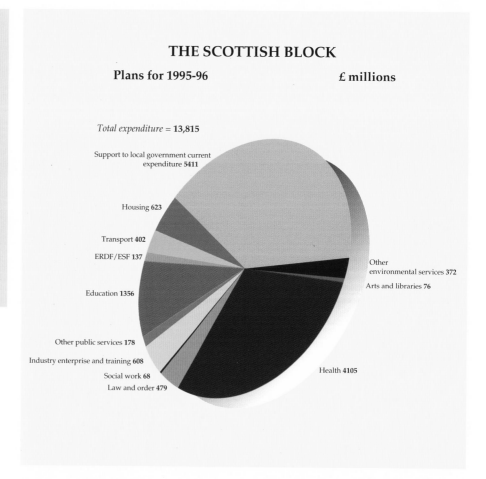

THE SCOTTISH BLOCK

Plans for 1995-96 £ millions

Total expenditure = 13,815

Support to local government current expenditure 5411
Housing 623
Transport 402
ERDF/ESF 137
Education 1356
Other public services 178
Industry enterprise and training 608
Social work 68
Law and order 479
Health 4105
Other environmental services 372
Arts and libraries 76

39 Rural Scotland has benefited over the years from public expenditure per head which, reflecting need, is greater than that committed to urban Scotland. This was a conclusion of a study carried out in 1985[7] and the indications are that this broad picture is still true today. Some types of support of particular importance in rural Scotland have increased substantially over the past ten years, notably direct payments to farmers and crofters. It has been the Government's aim to ensure that public expenditure is directed to priority areas and policies where value for money can be demonstrated. One effect of this has been that resources have been directed towards rural areas in recognition of the special problems they face such as a sparse population, remoteness, and other indicators of disadvantage. We will continue to ensure that the needs of rural Scotland are taken fully into account in future decisions on public expenditure.

Scottish Water and Sewerage Authorities

40 On 1 April 1996, the three new Scottish Water and Sewerage Authorities will take over responsibility for these services from local authorities and the Water and Sewerage Customers' Council will be established to look after the interests of consumers. Rural customers have a special place in these arrangements. The new authorities have a statutory duty to have particular regard to the interests of rural dwellers; the Secretary of State, in making appointments to the Customers Council, will seek to ensure that rural interests are represented; and same duty applies to the Customers Council when it make appointments to the three committees which it will establish, one for each of the new water authority areas.

Rural Water and Sewerage Grants

We fully recognise the high costs of infrastructure in rural areas. In particular, the earlier system of grants has been successful in stimulating the provision of water and sewerage services in rural areas. In place of the grant scheme, we have placed on the new Water Authorities a specific duty to have regard especially to the interests of rural customers and we will take account of this duty in providing resources to the Authorities. Thus the interests of rural customers will be central to the arrangements for service provision put in place by the authorities. We will review the effectiveness of these arrangements after the first year of operation.

HOUSING

Strathfillan

Our Housing Policy

The Government's overall aim is that a decent home should be within reach of every family in Scotland - whether they live in a rural or urban area. We have four strategic objectives in place to achieve that aim, these are:

● to promote greater housing choice

● to assist and enable provision of an adequate supply of housing

● to promote improvement in housing quality

● to seek more effective use of resources.

41 While our basic aim is the same for urban or rural Scotland, we know that there are particular housing problems in rural areas. These include: the scattered nature of settlements; the distances involved which increase

costs; the extreme weather conditions which contribute to poor conditions, especially dampness; the tenure pattern and, in some parts, pressure from second home buyers and commuters which tends to restrict the supply of affordable housing. We also recognise that while applications under the homelessness legislation are generally lower in rural than in urban areas, rural areas have particular problems, such as the use of residential caravans, often in poor repair, and holiday accommodation being available only for winter lets.

42 Substantial resources have been made available to address the special problems of housing in rural areas. We have made sure that rural local authorities receive a greater share of the resources available for council housing compared to the scale of their housing stock. Since 1979, rural local authorities have been allocated £1,669 million for public sector investment. For 1995-96, with just over 23% of the total housing stock, rural local authorities were allocated 25.5% or £108 million of the resources available for public sector investment. Since 1979 they have received £500 million for private sector housing investment. For 1995-96, with only 29% of the Scottish population, they were allocated £37 million. Since its inception in 1989, Scottish Homes has invested over £329 million in rural areas providing over 9,000 new or improved homes. In 1995-96 it plans to invest over £60 million to provide over 1,700 homes.

Scottish Homes

43 We asked Scottish Homes, as one of its first priorities after it was set up in 1989, to draw up a policy to address the rural housing challenge. In 1990, following extensive consultation involving a series of meetings run by Rural Forum and detailed research, Scottish Homes published its policy document *"The Role of Scottish Homes in Rural Scotland"*, which identified the need for new approaches to tackling rural housing issues and was seen as part of a move towards a more effective and better integrated policy for rural areas.

44 An innovative approach to address the challenge of rural housing was needed. Underlying the whole approach are the two important principles of supporting economic development and working in partnership with other agencies and local communities. Scottish Homes seeks to implement its policies in ways which are sympathetic to and supportive of rural communities and which create sustainable investment. For example, it:

- created 10 *Rural Demonstration Areas* to try out existing policy mechanisms and demonstrate new techniques. The Demonstration Areas have been evaluated and it was recommended that Scottish Homes continue to pilot new instruments and initiatives. This led to a range of innovative projects throughout rural Scotland which will continue testing new approaches;

- developed *Local Housing Agencies*, which are private sector organisations set up to provide specified housing services in a local area on behalf of Scottish Homes to provide more localised service delivery. Two agencies are being piloted - Tighean Innse Gall in the Western Isles and Eildon Housing Association in the Borders.

Scottish Homes
THE NATIONAL HOUSING AGENCY

Scottish Homes

The key objectives of Scottish Homes rural policy are to:

- increase housing supply

- improve housing conditions

- ensure affordability

- encourage residents' participation

Local Authorities

45 Local authorities also have an important role to play in meeting the rural housing challenge. Often they are working in partnership with Scottish Homes in implementing its rural housing policy. For their own investment under the system of Housing Plans, local authorities are required to draw up strategies and set targets in respect of local priority issues and the four identified national priority issues:

- **homelessness;**

- **condensation and dampness;**

- **below tolerable standard housing;**

- **community care.**

46 Authorities are required to assess their progress against these targets on an annual basis. Rural local authorities are responding to the new system and the main features of local authority housing investment in rural areas are works of energy efficiency to combat condensation and dampness in the public sector and a substantial improvement and repairs grant programme to combat the high incidence of below tolerable standard housing in both owner-occupied and tied houses. Increasingly, local authorities are looking to partnership with housing associations and other private sector partners to tackle their housing need.

47 Action on community care and homelessness should take account of rural problems and solutions for example, people living in residential caravans and housing and community care packages that enable people to live in their own homes rather than move into supported housing in the larger towns. Extra capital allocations have been given for such projects as reducing the use of residential caravans while care and repair schemes assist the elderly and disabled people to carry out repairs and adaptations allowing them to stay in their own home.

48 We also strongly encourage local authorities to consider stock transfers to housing associations as a means of improving the stock by opening up access to private finance. We look to local authorities and Scottish Homes to work in partnership to secure satisfactory housing provision. This will mean that resources are more effectively used, promoting an increased contribution from private funds, promoting better use of vacant or under used housing and promoting the co-ordination of housing and economic investment programmes designed to stimulate growth through the enterprise network.

Expanding Owner Occupation in Rural Areas

49 Our policy of increasing opportunities for home ownership has been successful in rural areas, as it has been across Scotland. Overall, home ownership has increased from 35% in 1979 to 57% in 1994 and is set to increase still further. We have set a target of 60% within the current Parliament. The *Right to Buy* is, of course, available to public sector tenants living in rural areas and many have taken advantage of the opportunity. Shared ownership schemes are also used extensively in rural areas and can be particularly beneficial in helping local people enter home ownership in pressurised housing markets. Rural Home Ownership Grants can also help people on modest incomes build their own home.

Promoting Scottish Local Government

The Condition of Rural Housing

The 1991 Scottish House Condition Survey showed:

- 6.6% of the occupied rural stock fell below the tolerable standard, compared with 4.3% in urban areas

- 18% of rural dwellings had rising or penetrating damp compared to 12% in urban areas

- Average repair costs were almost double the figure for urban areas

- 42% of rural properties needed repairs costing £1,000 or more compared to 29% of urban dwellings

- 36% of rural dwellings were built before 1919 compared to 18% of urban dwellings.

Scottish Homes Grants

Scottish Homes offers a range of grant mechanisms to increase the housing supply and to ensure affordability in rural areas:

● *Housing Association Grant*, the principal instrument for meeting the needs of the lower income groups in rural Scotland. We recognise that housing associations have a key role to play in meeting housing needs in rural areas. The majority of Scottish Homes investment in rural Scotland is through Housing Association Grant which remains the mainstay of affordable housing provision and is targeted at needy rural communities, based on local housing market and needs research. In 1995-96, grants to a network of over 20 rural and island housing associations will provide 800 houses for rent and 290 for shared ownership.

● *GRO grants for owner occupation* are designed to encourage the private sector to supply good quality new or improved homes in priority areas for investment. These areas now cover most of rural Scotland. Amongst the priorities are projects which provide housing for owner occupation, at affordable prices in areas where the supply is limited, or is constrained by market forces. A normal requirement of GRO grant is that council tenants and those on the waiting list are given priority in purchasing the homes. As well as enabling local people to get on to the home ownership ladder for whom it would not otherwise be possible, the scheme also frees up accommodation for those in housing need and relieves pressure on waiting lists.

● *Rural Home Ownership Grants*, which were piloted in the Western Isles, are targeted at individuals to assist them in gaining access to owner-occupation by helping them to build a new house or renovate an existing one. They have proved to be a cost-effective mechanism for providing low cost housing in remote areas. The grants were extended to all of rural Scotland last year and re-launched with new guidance, promotional material and a targeted leaflet campaign. Scottish Homes had awarded over 150 Rural Home Ownership Grants up to the end of 1994-95 and aims to award a further 120 in 1995-96.

50 Our policy of encouraging private sector provision has also paid dividends with private sector completions rising steadily in rural areas over the past decade. Almost 50,000 new homes have been built in rural areas since 1985. In 1994, a record year for private house building in Scotland, over 6,000 new homes were completed by private developers in rural areas, a significantly higher proportion per head of the population than in urban areas.

Making the Most of the Stock

51 Empty property is a matter of serious concern since it represents a wasted resource which could be brought back into use for those in housing need. Scottish Homes has a number of initiatives aimed at bringing empty houses back into use but of particular relevance to rural areas is the *Rural Empty Homes Initiative*. This started as a pilot in the Angus Glens Rural Demonstration Area and established that there was potential for bringing empty properties on estates back into use, with grant assistance from Scottish Homes for rehabilitation. Nine such grants were awarded in the pilot - not many, but even enabling one or two families to remain, or come

to live, in an area can make all the difference to the viability of the local school or the village shop. The scheme has been expanded throughout rural Scotland.

52 Rural local authorities generally have a lower level of empty houses than their urban counterparts. There are a number of reasons for this. They may have an attractive housing stock, with few houses which are difficult to let. Most do not face the problems of urban regeneration, under which blocks of flats or whole estates may be empty, awaiting comprehensive redevelopment and refurbishment, or even demolition.

Local authority housing, Mallaig

53 Nevertheless, rural authorities should seek to ensure that they reduce the number of empty houses to an absolute minimum. In October 1994, we published a *Good Practice Note on Void Management* which described a range of actions that landlords can take to reduce the number of empty houses. The Note points out that a pro-active management policy will minimise rent lost through property lying empty and it makes specific recommendations. These recommendations are relevant for rural authorities, which should use them to make sure that houses which are being vacated are reoccupied quickly by people in housing need.

54 We will continue to encourage rural local authorities and Scottish Homes to work together along with other partners such as housing associations, local enterprise companies, the private rented sector and local communities to meet the local housing challenge and to ensure that the specific housing needs of rural areas are taken into account at all levels.

COMMUNITY CARE

55 One of the key principles behind the Government's community care policy is that, where practicable, vulnerable people should be enabled to live in their own homes. In rural areas, where hospitals, residential care homes and nursing homes may be distant, home-based support may be the only way of assisting people to remain in the areas with which they are familiar.

Eday Village Hall, Orkney

56 There are practical problems with supporting people in their own homes where family and friends may not be close by and other community services may not be conveniently accessible. Innovative solutions can help meet the need. For example, the employment of local people, including neighbours, as home helps can support vulnerable people while bringing employment to others. Mobile units can allow a local hall or community centre to be converted into a day centre reducing travel costs and time.

57 The Day Access Rural Tayside mobile day centre is one of a number of projects which assist people with mental health problems and living in rural areas which are funded through the Mental Illness Specific Grant. This grant also supports a Hospital at Home project in Shetland which offers emergency, terminal and long-tern care services to people in their own homes. Another example is the Rural South Lanarkshire Corridor, managed by the Lanarkshire Association of Mental Health, which operates a number of advice and contact drop-in points, as well as outreach and home support services to assist people with mental health problems to integrate into the community.

58 Housing authorities should work closely with other housing bodies, and health and social work agencies, to ensure that housing and support services delivered to community care users is suited to local circumstances, particularly in sparsely populated areas. For instance, providing sheltered housing with in-house wardens only in the larger towns has the disadvantage of taking elderly people away from family and friends who provide informal support, and elderly people may therefore be reluctant to move to such accommodation.

59 Housing bodies should explore the options for more local provision, for example amenity housing for the elderly, linked to social work facilities rather than sheltered housing. Similar approaches may be appropriate for other community care client groups, including the provision of day care and other services in existing community facilities, and transport to them where this is cost effective.

DELIVERING HEALTH CARE IN RURAL AREAS

60 Provision of health care in rural areas in Scotland presents particular challenges. These are being met by the changes that are taking place in the NHS as a whole and by specific measures targeted at rural and island areas. A key role of Health Boards is to assess the needs of the local population and to purchase care to meet those needs. As a result, innovative ways of providing services close to the homes of people are being developed which are less dependent on what is provided in the local general hospital. This offers the potential for major benefits in rural areas which are some distance from such hospitals. To take forward this approach, all Health Boards prepared strategies for the development of primary care services during 1994. A report on health care services in remote and island areas in Scotland, prepared by the former Scottish Health Service Advisory Council, was issued earlier this year.

61 In addition, the General Practitioner fundholding scheme offers all family doctors, including those in rural areas, scope to provide additional services for their patients in the community and to improve the quality of hospital services. A number of GP practices in rural Scotland have taken advantage of the scheme to secure the provision of outreach services from hospitals in their practices. GP practices are also actively engaged with NHS Trusts in extending the range of services available from local community or cottage hospitals. These developments are facilitated by modern technology that enables conditions that previously required hospital admission to be treated by GPs or on a day-case basis. The new science of "tele-medicine" means that specialist diagnosis and advice can be obtained over a video link between the GP's surgery and the hospital.

62 Changes in the GP fundholding scheme, to come into effect on 1 April 1996, will benefit rural areas. For example, the size of patient lists needed for a practice to enter the standard fundholding scheme will be reduced, and a new option, called primary care purchasing, open to all practices regardless of list size, will enable many of the small practices in rural areas to participate.

63 The Government recognises that provision of services in rural areas gives rise to higher costs. As well as taking sparsity into account in its overall allocations to Health Boards, there are various specific payments. A Scottish Rural Practices Fund, amounting to over £5.5 million in 1995-96, compensates GPs for the higher costs arising from the scattered nature of their practices and the time spent in visiting patients living at a distance. Inducement payments are made to GPs practising in areas where it has been agreed that it is essential to maintain a medical practice; and help is given to single-handed practitioners to employ an associate GP to give them the opportunity for regular time-off and training in situations where continuous on-duty is otherwise inescapable. Dentists and opticians also receive special payments for visits to remote areas.

64 Patient transport in rural areas also poses problems because of the distances involved. Whilst road ambulances remain the first line of response, the Scottish Ambulance Service has pioneered the first integrated air ambulance

The National Health Service in Scotland

The NHS works to improve the health of the people of Scotland by:

● promoting better health

● helping to prevent illness

● providing the best treatment possible to those who are ill and health care for those with continuing needs

In delivering these objectives, it aims to:

● make sure that everyone who uses the NHS is treated as an individual

● improve access to services

● achieve value for taxpayer's money

These objectives apply throughout Scotland, although the way in which they are delivered varies according to many factors, including the geography and distribution of population across the country.

service in the UK with 3 helicopters and 4 fixed-wing aircraft. There are also schemes to assist patients in meeting the costs of travelling to hospital.

65 By maintaining and improving access to health services for people living in rural and island areas, the NHS is contributing to the viability of rural communities in all parts of Scotland.

Keeping the Shop Open

The Government intends to bring forward a scheme to reduce the burden of rates on the village shop which is providing a service to isolated communities.

Post Office Services

In 1994, it was agreed that Post Office Counters limited should offer the services of its network of 20,000 Post offices to a wider range of clients. This policy has led to a diversification of the services provided through local Post Offices. A number of new services, such as bureaux de change, travel insurance, and the free payment of gas bills have developed alongside the more traditional uses of Post Offices such as sale of postage stamps, and the point of access for the Royal Mail (including ParcelForce), the National Savings Bank, and the Benefits Agency. Post Offices are now the largest retailer of National Lottery tickets. These activities should help strengthen the network of Post Offices, not least those in rural areas.

An essential principle of the Royal Mail postal services is that of uniform delivery cost across the United Kingdom. This principle is of obvious importance to Scotland, and it remains unchanged in plans for the development of the Royal Mail.

THE VILLAGE SHOP

Ballinluig Post Office, Tayside

66 For many people, the village shop is one of the defining characteristics of the rural community. Even when the community is too small to support a pub, a church or a school it will have a shop and still be a recognisable village. It provides an essential service, often stocking an enormous variety of goods, and providing a range of services. It is often also the community meeting place, a local landmark and a centre to what otherwise may be a quite dispersed community.

67 But it has to be remembered that the shop is also a livelihood for the shopkeeper. Many rural shopkeepers feel that the burden of non-domestic rates is a significant threat to their continued viability. There is supporting evidence in recent research carried out for the Department of the Environment in respect of England. This shows that, while for most businesses rate bills are small in relation to total turnover, they impose a more substantial burden on the smallest businesses, particularly retail ones. We believe that a similar situation exists in Scotland.

68 We see no case for subsidising the general run of shops which fail to attract sufficient custom to remain viable. However, the small general store or post office in a rural village has a special social function. It often provides an invaluable, and irreplaceable, service for local people without cars or ready access to public transport. Its demise would be a severe blow to the community.

69   We therefore intend to introduce, at a suitable legislative opportunity, a new rate relief scheme targeted specifically on general stores and post offices in villages. We will consult widely on the technical details, but meanwhile we envisage that, to qualify for consideration, the shop would need to satisfy a number of conditions as to location, size, purpose and importance to the local community. It would not, however, be necessary to demonstrate that the ratepayer was suffering hardship.

70   In most parts of rural Scotland, local authority surveys have shown that there is a continuing decline in local services. The post office, the shop, primary school, doctor's surgery and petrol station are often mentioned as being of importance, with the village shop and primary school chief among them. The absence of these facilities can dissuade people from moving into an area and their closure can have serious effects on people's lives. Joint use of local facilities, such as the local school, library, shop or post office must be encouraged. As a practical example, Tayside Regional Council has set up a monitoring system of changes in five basic rural services to provide early warning of closures. Several regional authorities operate village shops schemes which offer advice and financial assistance for training, legal costs, improving premises and the quality of service to customers.

71   We published a draft National Planning Policy Guideline in 1995 which suggested that:

"the importance of village shops should be taken into account by planning authorities when faced with applications for new development or the change of use of existing shops. But ultimately local and village shops will remain viable only when suitable discount arrangements can be obtained from wholesalers and where people who shop there now continue to do so".

The National Lottery

72   Launched in November 1994, the National Lottery aims to create a new source of funding for the arts, sport, our natural heritage, charities and projects to mark the beginning of the new millennium. Through the distributing bodies, the Millennium Commission, the Scottish Sports Council, the Scottish Arts Council, and Historic Scotland it helps to fund projects which are for the public good and which benefit the community. Both rural and urban areas will benefit from the distribution of funds.

THE NATIONAL LOTTERY™

73   Many shops, garages and sub-post offices in rural areas are already selling National Lottery tickets, or will be doing so by the end of 1996 when Camelot plans to complete its network of around 40,000 retailers. With ticket sales continuing to run ahead of expectations, and retailers entitled to a commission of 5% on all sales, it is clear that this will bring considerable additional revenue to shopkeepers throughout the country, including in rural areas. In some cases, this might mean the difference between a shop remaining economically viable or having to close down.

74   The Director General of the National Lottery has directed Camelot to ensure that there is at least one Lottery retailer in every local authority

area, but, in practice, it is likely that many more terminals than this bare minimum requirement will be introduced, so that nobody will have to travel too far to be able to take part in the National Lottery.

National Lottery Successes

Scottish projects with a rural aspect have already benefited from the Lottery. Some examples are:

● The SUSTRANS cycle network, which plans to link Inverness to Dover with a wide network of cycle tracks was awarded £42.5 million in September 1995.

● The Arran Theatre and Arts Trust at Brodick benefited to the extent of £609,000.

● Shetland Folk Festival Society received £5,000

● The Plockton Village Hall was given over £62,000.

● The Bennachie Community Centre at Insch is to receive £311,000.

● The Millennium Forest for Scotland Trust, which brings the benefits of forestry to a new audience altogether, was awarded £5.75 million in October 1995. This will enable 45 projects to go ahead, aimed at extending the cover of native woodlands and improving public access to woodland in Scotland.

SCOTTISH CULTURE

The Arts & Crafts

75 In all civilised societies the arts have an intrinsic value and this is as true of rural communities as it is of urban. Increasingly too, the social, economic, and environmental impact of the arts is being recognised and funding partnerships between local authorities, economic development agencies, and arts funding bodies have been established within rural communities to develop and sustain a thriving cultural sector.

76 The arts benefit rural areas in diverse ways. They have an impact on increasing rural population through attracting artists and their families and by retaining people active within a community who might move away without the social and cultural stimulation provided by a lively arts environment. The arts also play a highly significant part in maintaining and raising awareness within a community of its traditions and identity. This is exemplified by a wide range of bodies dedicated to traditional music including pipe bands, accordion and fiddle clubs, folk clubs, traditional dance societies in all their rich diversity - ample evidence of the popularity of the traditional musical arts. Further evidence is found in the many Highland games and the wide range of local festivals and events held throughout Scotland. Clearly the arts also have a crucial role in helping to define and develop contemporary culture. Many festivals such as those at Dunkeld and Pittenweem blend traditional and contemporary arts most effectively, while theatres such as the Pitlochry Festival Theatre, the Byre Theatre at St Andrews, and Eden Court at Inverness bring a blend of classical and contemporary drama to their areas. All such events play their part in defining and providing a focus for the rural community.

Sculpture, near Langholm

77 In economic terms, the arts contribute, directly and indirectly, to the creation and retention of new employment and the role of the arts in improving the image of an area both for visitors and for potential businesses should not be underestimated. There is, of course, an obvious interface between arts and tourism: a study undertaken in 1989 showed that the arts tourism market was worth £40 million a year to Scotland.

78 Crafts represent a significant sector of the small business economy in many rural areas. A socio-economic report, *"Crafts in the 1990s"* published by the Crafts Council in 1994 indicates that there was a 75% increase in crafts people working in Scotland between 1981 and 1992. The crafts sector plays a significant role in tourism development in rural areas, differentiating localities and adding quality and diversity to the range of attractions on offer.

79 The arts have an environmental impact on rural areas. Commissioned works can be used to interpret natural surroundings and enhance the enjoyment of landscape, and can help raise awareness of environmental issues. One example is the Tyrebagger Sculpture Project in Kirkhill Forest in Aberdeenshire where the unveiling of five specially commissioned sculptures in June 1994 marked the inauguration of a long-term project designed to create a community, as well as a major cultural destination, for visitors to the North East.

80 Government funding for the arts in Scotland is directed through the Scottish Arts Council. The Council and other cultural agencies are working together with local authorities, public agencies, the private and voluntary sectors to devise ways in which relevant and quality service can be delivered. An Arts and Tourism Task Force has been established in partnership with the Scottish Tourist Board, Scottish Arts Council, Scottish Enterprise, and other bodies. The Council has also co-funded arts development posts in rural areas with local authorities and development agencies, and has provided support for cultural agencies working in rural areas, for example Arts in Fife, Dumfries and Galloway Arts Association and Seall Community Arts in Skye.

Mel Gibson and Michael Forsyth
celebrating the première of
"Braveheart"

The Scottish Film Industry: Film and Television

Scotland has much to offer international film makers. The beauty and variety of the Scottish landscape and the ease of communications in an English-speaking country are just some of the factors that have attracted film producers to shoot films in Scotland. Indeed, two of the most successful Hollywood movies of 1995, "Rob Roy" and "Braveheart" had scenes shot in the Scottish Highlands. The benefits which film and television production can bring to local economies is recognised by the Government, as is the potential to use films shot in Scotland to promote Scotland as a tourist venue.

This is something which the Government wishes to see developed and to this end The Scottish Office has recently asked Scottish Enterprise and Highlands and Islands Enterprise to commission work to identify, and help overcome, constraints to the future development of the media industry in Scotland. The Scottish Office has also commissioned the Scottish Film Council to produce a CD-ROM to give film makers from all over the world access to information about Scotland and it is hoped that this will prove to be an effective marketing tool in encouraging overseas producers to Scotland.

The setting up in 1993 of the Scottish Office financed Gaelic Television Fund has already helped develop television production throughout the Highlands and Islands. Grampian TV, for example, has established a small studio complex in Stornoway which employs 15 staff. In addition, Scottish Television has taken a conscious decision to record their major Gaelic drama series "Machair" on location in the Western Isles and, by doing so, they have created quality jobs on the Islands and production has significantly boosted the Islands' economy. The Fund has also helped small independent producers establish their businesses in the Highlands where currently there are three independent producers working in the Western Isles and two in Skye.

Gaelic

81 Gaelic culture is important to many people in the rural areas of north west Scotland. In addition to its linguistic importance, it represents a distinct cultural identity and a way of life, relating in particular to crofting. Recent years have witnessed a revival of interest in Gaelic as shown, for example, by the popularity across the country of Gaelic music groups such as *"Capercaillie"* and *"Runrig"*. The revival of interest in learning language is reflected in the number of playgroups, schools and adult education classes now offering courses. The first Gaelic playgroup opened in 1982 and by 1995 there were over 50 playgroups operating throughout the Highlands and Islands. The growth in the playgroup movement has also mirrored a growth in the provision of education through the medium of Gaelic and currently there are some 50 Gaelic medium primary units providing education for some 1,300 pupils.

82 The Gaelic college on Skye, Sabhal Mor Ostaig, is a leading force in the upsurge of interest in the Gaelic culture and language. The college employs 24 people and acts as a base for conferences and other events as well as providing full-time and short courses for students and Gaelic learners. It is a major contributor to the vitality of the Sleat peninsula. Through its

Community Radio

The smallest independent radio station in Britain,"Heartland Radio", covers almost 3,000 square kilometres of Highland Perthshire and offers a service to a potential audience of some 5,500. The station's programmes are produced and presented by volunteers and since its inception in 1992 the station has built up a loyal local audience for its output which includes local voices, local current affairs and Scots originated music of all sorts. The success of "Heartland" has demonstrated that radio stations of this kind can do much to create a community spirit in rural areas.

Throughout Scotland there are many rural communities which aspire to following "Heartland". Some groups have applied to the Radio Authority (the public body charged with issuing licences for commercial broadcasting in the United Kingdom) for a restricted broadcasting licence which enables them to broadcast for a few days or weeks each year to enhance seasonal events, raise consciousness about a project, issue, or opportunity or simply to boost community confidence and foundries in an enjoyable manner. One such group in Stornoway found that their restricted licence service was so popular that they were able to persuade the Radio Authority that a permanent broadcasting licence for a community station in the area should be advertised.

Permanent stations now planned for Oban and Peterhead will join stations already on air in a number of locations through the Scottish Highlands, many of which have received financial assistance with capital costs from local enterprise companies. The Government welcomes the development of community radio in Scotland and recognises the valuable contribution it can make towards developing community life in rural areas[8].

subsidiary companies Cannan (a Gaelic publishing company) and Leirsinn (a research company) it has become a major employer in the area.

83 Skye is not the only area to benefit from employment related to the promotion of the Gaelic language and culture. Recent research commissioned by Highlands and Islands Enterprise and Comunn na Gaedhlig (the Gaelic development agency) showed that in 1993 there were almost 1,000 full-time equivalent jobs involved in some way with the promotion and development of the language and culture which contributed some £41 million to Scotland's gross domestic product.

Public Libraries

84 Public libraries are central to the cultural activity of rural communities through provision of services which contribute to the educational, information and leisure needs of the populations which they serve and local authorities have a statutory duty to secure the provision of adequate public library facilities for the residents of their areas. In addition to offering access to a wide range of arts-related material, literature, music, videos and information services, libraries are often a centre for community arts activities through promotion of cultural events and provision of facilities for groups and societies fostering the creative use of leisure through the arts. Mobile libraries can provide a vital service to rural communities.

Crofting museum, Skye

Museums

85 Like libraries, museums are ideal venues and resources for arts and cultural activities, both educational and recreational, and in rural areas they can help to provide a sense of community and local cohesion. They also have considerable impact on local and national economic development, particularly in the area of tourism, where they can bring added value to visits to rural areas. A number of Museums Forums, which are self-help networking groups charged with raising standards in a cluster of museums, particularly in geographically fragmented and remoter areas, have been established and good examples of these are found in the Borders, Highlands and Islands and Shetland.

Crofting museum, Skye

THE FUTURE FOR SCOTTISH RURAL COMMUNITIES

86   It would be easy to concentrate on the jobs and economy of rural Scotland. But our rural communities have a rich and varied life which too has to be celebrated. The mood in much of the world is to recapture the diversity of our many different communities, not to turn the clock back but as a way of invigorating rural life. Improving housing, enabling people to live in the communities they have know all their lives, educating our children for living in the broad Scottish tradition; these are all important matters to be pushed forward alongside the search for prosperity.

87   We need to work towards the development of regional identities; where each society, each group, each person, is able to express their character. Man will always wish to explore change, to grasp opportunities, to seek a higher quality of life. The impetus for change can very often arise from aspirations identified more with urban issues and communities.

88   This document outlines a general policy framework which enables rural communities to move forward. We are determined that the people of these communities should be enabled to take control of their lives, with the assistance of networks of experienced organisations, to to meet challenges and seize the opportunities.

SCOTLAND'S
WORKING
LANDSCAPE

89 We have concentrated, so far, on the ways in which rural people live and the action the Government takes to enable them to make the most of the opportunities available. Against competing pressures, we need to enable the countryside to continue to fulfil its role as a working landscape offering life and work for the communities which made it. Those who live in the countryside are acutely aware of its importance to others, in providing a place for recreation, an escape from the noise and congestion of the city and, most importantly, as the place most associated with landscape and wildlife. They wish to use it, enhance it as well as protect it in order to have something of which they can be proud in handing it on to their children.

90 It is a task for Government to recognise these pressures and bring them to the attention of all interested parties with a view to resolving conflict. In this we are guided by the fundamental principles which we set out in our White Paper on the Environment, " This Common Inheritance"[8]. Each year we have published a report on how the programme we set out has been progressed. At its heart are two primary concerns that:

- **we should proceed as far as possible without compulsion or the force of law, under the voluntary principle;**

- **our ultimate goal is sustainable development, living in a manner which does not constrain the options open to our descendants.**

91 To do this we need to take forward policies on a broad front, each working to its sectoral purpose, within overall concerns for people and planet.

SUSTAINABLE DEVELOPMENT

92 At the 1992 United Nations Conference of Environment and Development, the "Earth Summit", the UK and over 150 other governments endorsed Agenda 21, a framework for action into the next century. This committed their countries to prepare national strategies for action to preserve local, national and global environments. Overall, these initiatives are concerned with the issue of the general management of the planet, summed up as *sustainable development*. We took a lead at the Earth Summit committing ourselves to make future development sustainable, not turning away from growth but ensuring that growth did not place an intolerable burden on future generations.

93 Sustainable development is not just a high-flown concept for international agencies; it is already being promoted in many different ways in the United Kingdom at national and local levels, in business and in homes. We are determined to apply it to our actions in all fields. Thus in our policies, such as those on planning, transport, housing and economic development, we are building in steps towards sustainable development. In 1994 we published the United Kingdom Strategy for Sustainable Development which sets out our programme of action. In some fields progress is in small steps, because the necessary changes to our actions are difficult; in others more rapid progress is becoming possible. Much work is underway on these issues and, in Scotland, the Secretary of State is advised directly by an eminent panel, the Advisory Group on Sustainable Development, which has a broad remit to look at sustainable development issues across the whole of Scotland.

SCOTTISH NATURAL HERITAGE

Scottish Natural Heritage

It aims to

● safeguard and enhance Scotland's natural heritage, particularly its natural, genetic and scenic diversity;

● promote enjoyment of, and responsible public access to, the natural heritage in ways which do not damage it;

● encourage public support and voluntary effort for the benefit of the environment;

● promote improvement of the natural heritage in and around towns and cities, where most of Scotland's people live

Scottish Natural Heritage declares as its basic philosophy:

"we must care for and sustain our natural heritage if we want it to sustain us. So we seek to promote the good management of the natural heritage so that we can pass it on, in a healthy and invigorated state, to succeeding generations. We seek to foster greater understanding and better practice through well-founded policies, through demonstration projects, through education and through partnerships which promote joint action."

94 Sustainable development cannot be achieved by Government alone. It calls for action by all. Local authorities have their own programme of action following the Rio Conference, known as Agenda 21. But changes in individuals' patterns of consumption and behaviour will also be necessary in the longer term - hence the importance of education and information on environmental issues. The Scottish Office published *"A Scottish Strategy for Environmental Education"* in 1995 and this is being taken forward by the Education for Sustainable Development Group, a sub-group of the Advisory Group on Sustainable Development.

PEOPLE AND NATURE

95 We have assembled a powerful group of policies and agencies to give effect to our objectives and obligations. In 1992 we created Scottish Natural Heritage, which was the first Government agency to have sustainable development as one of its primary concerns and are now establishing the Scottish Environment Protection Agency which will also have to take account of sustainable development in its work. Scottish Natural Heritage has a responsibility to look to the interests of the wider countryside. It seeks to enable people, of all interests and abilities, to enjoy the countryside.

Our Responsibilities to the Natural Heritage

96 The Government has significant obligations to the protection and enhancement of our natural heritage. We have entered fully into the growing movement, worldwide, to take action to preserve and enhance the natural heritage, and this continues action which we have been pursuing for many years. In so doing we have joined with our European partners to put in place arrangements for protection of species and habitats, through such measures as the Natura 2000 network, which is the practical expression of the 1979 EC Birds Directive[9] and the 1992 EC Habitats Directive[10] . Having signed the Biodiversity Convention[11] at the Earth Summit in Rio, the United Kingdom became one of the first countries to produce a biodiversity strategy in January 1994. The Action Plan commits us to:

● **seek to conserve and where possible enhance wild species and wildlife habitats;**

- ensure that all policy areas respect and integrate these concerns;

- increase awareness and involvement in conserving biodiversity.

97 We have contributed fully to the 1995 European Year of Nature Conservation. Scottish Natural Heritage has a full programme of events to mark the year which is intended to press home to everyone the importance of nature conservation, not just for the intrinsic interest of wildlife but because it is the vital resource on which much of our rural economy is based.

Using the Countryside

98 In planning for sustainable development we have to bear in mind that significant changes cannot be made overnight. In the countryside, in particular, much change has to follow the natural calendar with its annual cycles of activity. Traditional activities, like agriculture, forestry, fishing and country pursuits on open moors have achieved their present form over many years, adjusting at a natural pace to changing circumstances and demands.

99 Many people come into the countryside simply for pleasure. They do so in a variety of ways, reflecting their interests and fitness: some come for an afternoon stroll ending at a tea shop, others seek to plunge deep into remote territory or to challenge a Munro or two. Some are tourists and rural communities benefit from their visit by providing accommodation, whether bed & breakfast or something more elaborate. Others relish travelling under their own steam and try hard to avoid the familiar well-trodden routes. In 1994, Scottish Natural Heritage published a consultation paper on access, *Enjoying the Outdoors*[12] which proposes *"Paths for All"* an initiative intended to improve access to the outdoors for all especially those in towns and cities.

Rannoch Moor, Glencoe

The Natura 2000 Network

- **Special Areas of Conservation:** The Habitats Directive lists habitats and species of animals which are important in the European Community because they are rare, endangered or vulnerable. 63 of those species and 52 habitats are found in Scotland, including 14 priority habitats.

- **Special Protection Areas:** With its rich variety of habitats, Scotland is a very special place for wild birds. Some are permanent residents, some come here to breed, some overwinter, some use Scotland as a staging post while migrating. Since these wild birds do not recognise national boundaries, we need international agreements to protect them. The 1979 EC Wild Birds Directive gives Member state of the European Community powers and responsibilities to classify Special Protection Areas to protect all regularly occurring migratory birds, and vulnerable birds which are listed in the Directive.

- **The Scottish Network:** The Government is consulting on the areas to be given these forms of protection.

The Land Cover of Scotland Survey

The first detailed census of the land cover of Scotland was begun in 1987 as a result of increasing concern about the nature and rate of change of land use in rural Scotland. The main objectives were to provide authoritative information for both policy and research purpose and to provide a baseline against which past and future change might be assessed. It has provided widely used data which can be linked to other surveys such as the Countryside Survey 1990.

100 But each visitor, whether local or tourist, leaves a mark on the countryside, every footstep on a path contributes to its erosion, continuing the pressure which man places on the natural heritage. Our commitment to the global issues wrapped up in sustainable development requires us to give careful thought to how we deal with these matters when they impact locally.

Wild Flowers, Skye

Partnership in Practice

101 In some areas a much broader view of protection, enhancement and the encouragement of sympathetic use needs to be taken. We have been convinced of the need for action in two such areas, the Cairngorms and in Loch Lomond & the Trossachs. These areas differ considerably from each other, both geographically and in the pressures which they experience. Each is home to some 15,000 people whose lives reflect those traditional patterns mentioned earlier. But no one form of management would suit both. We have therefore made it plain what action is needed and have taken it forward.

102 We are proud of our mountain areas and for the most part the careful stewardship offered by the local landowners, with the assistance and advice of statutory bodies such as the Red Deer Commission and Scottish Natural Heritage, provides appropriate management. However, we accepted advice that the Cairngorms requires a different approach. The *Cairngorms Partnership* started work in earnest in April 1995. It is almost exactly the body recommended by the Report of the Cairngorms Working Party and has, on its Board, representatives of all the local authorities in the area, both existing and new, as well as members who represent such interest groups as environmentalists, landowners, tourist and recreational users.

103 It is a private sector organisation, separated from Government and drawing its power and influence from the organisations which have agreed to join it. A lead was given by the Secretary of State[13] in appointing its first Chairman and identifying priorities and tasks which needed to be addressed early in its work programme. Its main task is to develop and implement a management strategy for the area but it will also consider the benefits which might come from designating a Natural Heritage Area. It will work towards a management arrangement which would enable the Cairngorms to complete the steps necessary to have it declared a World Heritage Site.

Red Deer, Morrone Birchwood, Braemar

104 In Loch Lomond & the Trossachs, we again accepted the main recommendations of a working party established to examine the area and its needs, and are looking to the local authorities in the area to come together in a joint committee which would take an integrated view of the management of the area. The pressures here are different to those facing the Cairngorms and we agree with the working party that the main elements of the management strategy can be achieved using existing local authority powers and functions. In each area, planning and tourist pressures will require careful handling, appropriate to the nature and scale of the problems.

105 We are not convinced by those who call for such areas to be brought into public ownership as the only way in which our heritage can be protected. To do so risks losing that rich variety of countryside which is part of the glory of Scotland and the costs would be a burden on many people whose opportunity to make use of the investment required would be very limited. We believe that the land of Scotland is well protected from hazard by the systems in place under both our international obligations and the arrangements, like the Sites of Special Scientific Interest and the National Nature Reserves, which we introduced almost 15 years ago. But land management is not simply about protection. Most areas need active management and it is in the interests of landowners to see that this is pursued with vigour. Scotland's landscape, however wild its appearance, is almost entirely the result of intervention by man. Having taken it in hand, it is the duty of the landowner to continue to protect and enhance the land in his charge.

106 A number of voluntary organisations provide fine examples of land management, in particular, the John Muir Trust and the National Trust for Scotland. The acquisition of the Mar Lodge Estate by the National Trust, with substantial assistance from the National Lottery Fund and others, has safeguarded a huge area of the Cairngorms but it should be noted that the sums of money involved were not far short of half the annual budget of Scottish Natural Heritage. In calling for the purchase of such land critics may need to consider the relative importance of one site against the broader objectives to be pursued.

Deer and Deer Management

There are an estimated 300,000 wild red deer in Scotland together with possibly a similar number of deer of other species, principally roe and sika. These deer are an important part of Scotland's natural heritage and deer stalking and the sale of venison provide valuable sources of income and employment in many parts of rural Scotland. Wild deer populations can, however, create damage to agricultural crops, woodlands and other aspects of the natural heritage and there is a need for careful management and, where necessary, control measures, to avoid these problems.

The Red Deer Commission has a key role to play in encouraging good deer management. It has powers to deal with marauding deer and it works closely with Deer Management Groups throughout the red deer range to encourage deer estate owners and other interested parties to take a co-ordinated approach. It also advises the Secretary of State on all matters relating to wild deer. In recent years, we have provided additional resources to allow the Commission to expand its activities, particularly in the south of Scotland.

We have announced proposals for amending and strengthening deer legislation in order to create a more flexible framework for action by the Commission and deer managers to tackle the problems caused by excessive deer numbers in parts of Scotland.

107 Some would see our outstanding natural heritage areas as demanding the arrangements available elsewhere for National Parks. At one level it is easy to understand the appeal of this but careful examination by the former Countryside Commission for Scotland and subsequent wide consultation did not provide convincing evidence that a statutory over-riding of existing authorities was justified. The Cairngorms and Loch Lomond & the Trossachs are indeed special, but it does not take a traveller long to realise that, jewels in the crown though they may be, there are many other gems across Scotland. Instead of continuing to designate large areas of the country as special, with the implication that those not so designated are less deserving of attention, we have sought, through Scottish Natural Heritage, to take a broader view of our responsibilities.

The Central Scotland Forest

The most ambitious environmental and landscape improvement project in Scotland is taking place in the countryside between Scotland's two largest cities. The purpose of the Secretary of State's Central Scotland Woodlands Initiative, launched in 1989, is to create a new woodland environment - a Central Scotland Forest - stretching from the foothills of the Campsies to the foothills of the Pentlands, and from the eastern fringes of Glasgow to the western fringes of Edinburgh taking in Falkirk, Cumbernauld and Livingston. The project aims to transform the degraded landscape of the Central Belt, and provide social and economic benefits, by the early part of the next century.

The Central Scotland Countryside Trust has the pivotal role in creating the Central Scotland Forest. The Trust is a wide ranging partnership embracing central Government, and its agencies, local authorities, the voluntary and private sectors all of which share the Initiative's common objectives, to provide the focus and vehicle for the development of the Forest.

Historically, The Scottish Office is the largest sponsor of the Trust. In 1995-96 it is making £850,000 available to the Trust; thus continuing its previously high level of support. In addition, the Forestry Commission, following consultation with the Trust, has this year introduced a grant supplement for priority areas in Central Scotland.

The Review of Designations:

The main aims will be to

- re-affirm importance of statutory designations, Natura 2000 and SSSI, and consider what needs to be done for landscape

- define relationships between them and offer guidance on use and impact

- await practical proposals from Cairngorms Partnership before moving forward with Natural Heritage Areas

- pursue simplification and de-regulation consistent with over-arching nature conservation objectives

Simplifying Designations

108 We recognise that the array of different natural heritage and related designations, which has been added to by recent European Directives, has now grown to the point where there is a real risk of confusion. In addition, a number of organisations, both local authority and non-governmental have used the concept of designation to draw attention to many environmental issues, especially those of local interest. Scottish Natural Heritage has done valuable ground work in its Task Force on Designations but we intend to carry through a review of designations in use in Scotland in order to clarify their purposes, define their impacts and, where possible, identify steps with de-regulation in mind, which will reduce the apparent burden implied by the range now in use.

THE WIDER ENVIRONMENT

The Scottish Environment Protection Agency

109 One of the main achievements of the Environment Act 1995, was to provide for the creation of the Scottish Environment Protection Agency. This will, from 1 April 1996, provide a single, integrated pollution control body with responsibility for land, air and water. Within that remit, the Agency will tackle a wide range of problems, from rural river pollution to factory emissions in the Central Belt. It is required, under its founding

statute, to have regard to the desirability of conserving and enhancing the natural heritage of Scotland, and will consult Scottish Natural Heritage about any of its activities which may adversely areas of special natural heritage or scientific interest. The new Agency will also be under a specific duty to have regard to the social and economic needs of any area of Scotland, and in particular to such needs of rural areas.

Pitlochry Hydro Dam

Renewable Energy

The Government is encouraging the development of renewable energy, where it has prospect of being economic and environmentally acceptable.

● Wind farms produce no harmful gases and create employment in rural areas. Advice has been given to local planning authorities. As a result of the Government decision to oblige the Scottish electricity supply companies to secure more electricity from sustainable sources, twelve wind projects have secured contracts from Scottish Power and HydroElectric Power.

● Coppice of willow or poplar can be grown in short rotations, using methods more commonly used for arable crops, and harvested every 2-4 years for fuel.

Planning for Rural Communities

110 One of the main ways in which the attractiveness of rural life is maintained and enhanced for future generations and in which opportunities are opened up is through the planning system. Through the strategic framework offered by the structure plans and the more detailed proposals which form the local plans communities can help define how they wish their areas to develop. The planning system depends heavily on consultation and incorporates process for achieving consensus or for resolving conflict should that arise.

111 Development Plans lie at the heart of the system. They are intended to identify the scope for new development and to outline the basis for development control. Development Plans are subject to periodic review when they can be adjusted to meet emerging needs and community preferences. Thus they evolve over time by identifying future needs, catering for those needs in an environmentally acceptable manner having regard to the rights of the individual and the objective of securing sustainable development.

112 The strands need to be woven together with considerable care when planning for rural communities. In recent years there has been population growth in some rural areas and lively rural communities will continue to seek to take advantage of new opportunities. It is however all too easy to

Opening Up Rural Opportunities

We will produce guidance on rural development intended to encourage positive provision for employment and community purposes using the development plan and control systems. The guidance, to be published in 1996, will offer ideas on:

● small businesses

● local added value

● conversion and re-use of existing buildings

● lowland crofting

● settlement pattern and transport issues

● community provision and participation.

We will also issue guidance during 1996 on planning for small towns in rural areas covering particularly:

● provision for regeneration and expansion town centres

● transport issues

● townscape quality

destroy the very environmental qualities which first attract people or development to an area. Establishing sustainable development for the long-term benefit of rural communities should therefore be a pre-requisite for those concerned with the preparation of Development Plans for such areas. While growth at any environmental cost is no longer acceptable, the creation of a healthy rural economy is a prime concern of Government and that should be reflected in the policies and proposals set out in Development Plans.

113 Providing opportunity in rural areas is essential but so too is the need to establish stability. Rural areas, particularly those on the urban fringe, are most vulnerable to speculative pressure. The Government has therefore long attached great importance to preserving existing green belts and to the need to establish confidence in their permanence. Stability and endurance of green belt policies can be expected only where a balance between containment and growth of development can be sustained on a long-term basis. Once again that is a matter for Development Plans and where appropriate subsequent structure plan submissions have addressed this issue.

Planning for Rural Opportunities

114 The planning system is already offering much to assist rural development. Guidance has been offered to local authorities on *"Development Opportunities and Local Plans"*[14] which included two examples from Highland and Borders regions, suggesting that local plans should be followed by a compendium of development opportunities which could be marketed widely. Advice has also been given on how to set about achieving environmentally acceptable development in rural areas. This has ranged from the design and location of farm and forestry buildings to the fitting of new housing development into the landscape.

Building on the Best of Scottish Design

115 As more people choose to live and stay in rural Scotland, including some of the remoter areas, concerns have been raised about the siting and design of some of the new houses which have been built. Only too often houses are sited without full regard for the sensitive Scottish landscape and built without reference to local traditions in terms of design features and materials. The result is to introduce, in an unthinking way, housing which is alien to the Scottish scene. What we build today will continue to have an impact on the quality of life for many generations. New housing in the countryside should not be thought of in isolation but should be designed to recognise and sit in harmony with its surroundings.

116 We have taken important steps to improve matters by issuing advisory technical publications[15] and are keen to see not only the worst examples of the past avoided but to invite people to come forward with house designs showing individual modern architecture of high quality. Initiatives such as the Saltire Society's design award for New Housing in Rural Areas have encouraged change for the better although there remains considerable scope for improvement.

Green Belts

Our long-term objectives for green belts are to:

● maintain the identification of towns by establishing a clear definition of their physical boundaries and preventing their coalescence;

● provide countryside for recreation of all kinds;

● maintain the landscape setting of towns.

A Rural Business Use Class

In order to ensure that the planning system continues to play its full part in business development the Government intend to include proposals for a Rural Business Use Class in the consultation on the Use Classes Order to be published in the autumn of 1995, which is part of the wider review of the Scottish planning system.

Clashnessie

117 They also want to see housing which takes account of the varied traditions of building design which have developed across Scotland in answer to differences in landscape character, climate and locally available materials. New housing should not be a pastiche of the past but rather an innovative interpretation that, whilst reflecting the best of these traditions, satisfies the demands of the present.

AGRICULTURE AND THE ENVIRONMENT

118 Farmers and crofters are responsible for managing some 75% of the land area of Scotland and they have a significant role as custodians of the countryside. The traditional landscapes and the rich variety of wildlife found in Scotland's countryside have been very largely shaped by the hand of farmers over the generations. The farming community also relies on the fertility of their soils and an adequate water supply for their crops and livestock and it well appreciates the need for stewardship of these vital natural resources.

119 We seek to help Scottish farmers and crofters to protect the environment and ensure careful use of natural resources by:

  ● **giving guidance on best practices in environmentally friendly farming, in particular through Codes of Practice on the:**
  - *Prevention of Environmental Pollution from Agricultural Activity*
  - *Safe Use of Pesticides on Farms*
  - *Good Upland Management*
  ● **supporting advice to the farmers and crofters on conservation and environmental management through the Scottish Agricultural College and the Farming and Wildlife Advisory Groups with**

The Scottish Agri-Environment Programme

This programme includes the following Schemes:

● *Environmentally Sensitive Areas:* a whole farm approach in which farmers and crofters are eligible to receive a range of payments for measures set out in an agreed conservation plan.

● *Organic Aid:* assistance for farmers and crofters who wish to convert to organic production methods.

● *Habitats:* payments to encourage farmers and crofters to establish specific habitats of particular conservation value by either agreeing to take the land out of production for 20 years or agreeing to use it for limited grazing only.

● *Heather Moorland:* payments to encourage hill farmers and crofters to reduce sheep stocking rates where this would help to encourage heather regeneration.

● *Set-Aside Access:* payments to encourage the use of set-aside land for quiet recreation.

Government financial assistance, channelled through Scottish Natural Heritage. The Farming and Wildlife Advisory Group has increased to 19 the number of local advisers throughout Scotland;

● funding an extensive programme of environmental research directed to understanding the interaction between agriculture and the environment.

Clipping sheep, Stoer

120 We recognise that there is a case for payments to be made to farmers and crofters where environmental benefits can be obtained from agricultural management which goes beyond the needs of good farming practice. We launched the Environmentally Sensitive Area (ESA) Scheme in 1987, initially in two areas of Scotland, to provide payments to farmers if they agreed to an integrated programme of conservation management and works on their land. Since then, the Government has used the Agri-Environment Regulation, which formed part of the 1992 reform of the Common Agricultural Policy, as the basis for expanding the ESA Scheme in Scotland so that it now operates in 10 separate areas and also covers 20% of the land area and to introduce a number of new schemes.

121 One cause for concern in the countryside is the use of pesticides. The Scottish Agricultural Science Agency contributes to the monitoring of pesticide levels carried out by the Working Party on Pesticide Residues, which supports the approvals process for pesticides. The Advisory Committee on Pesticides offers advice on the safety of pesticides when Ministers are considering approvals. We are committed to minimise the use of pesticides through the use of these rigorous approval procedures, through guidance to users and through research and development and are working towards guidance on guidance on integrated pest and crop management.

122 Since 1988, farmers have been able to obtain capital grants for environmentally beneficial investments such as hedge planting and the repair and re-instatement of stone dykes and vernacular buildings through the *Farm and Conservation Grant Scheme*. The Government considers that there may be scope for integrating this Scheme more closely with the Scottish Agri-Environment Programme with the aim of extending the range of conservation incentives available to farmers and crofters in Scotland. Work is currently in hand on the development of proposals which would provide the framework for a comprehensive and integrated conservation scheme which would also contribute to the rationalisation of the agri-environment programme. Subject to the availability of resources, the Government will consult on its proposals for a new Scheme.

Forestry, Elibank

Country Sports

123 Much of our apparently wild landscape has been shaped by those who over the last couple of centuries have come to enjoy country sports. Often our moors and forests are the direct result of investment by landowners, who in past times may have earned that money furth of Scotland. These working landscapes are the envy of the world and, while the sports enjoyed may not be to the taste of all, it cannot be denied that without that care and investment our wildlife might very well not be nurtured as it is today. Once again, those landscapes can bring benefits to a wider community. Studies have shown that field sports support a considerable tourist business, with shooting alone accounting for over 50,000 visitors in 1988. Angling for salmon and trout makes an important contribution to the economy, particularly in rural areas. These fisheries, particularly those for salmon, have an international reputation which attracts fishermen far and wide. In 1992 the total contribution of British sportsmen in 1992 to the Scottish economy is estimated at £40 million with half as much again coming from overseas.

Forestry and the Environment

● The Forestry Commission's environmental guidelines, covering nature conservation, landscape, water, recreation and archaeology, set standards for the forestry industry:

● where forestry activities are likely to have a significant environmental impact, landowners are required to prepare an environmental statement.

● the Forestry Commission has well-established procedures for consulting local authorities and Scottish Natural Heritage on applications for new forestry and for felling woodlands.

● indicative forestry strategies provide a framework for balancing environmental priorities with proposals for new forestry.

Indicative Forestry Strategies

● We offered guidance to Regional and Island Councils in 1990 on the preparation of Indicative Forestry Strategies which sought to encourage the expansion of forestry in a manner which respected the environment. Strategies identified the main areas of opportunity for new planting and areas where there might be constraints to planting and provided a framework for consultation.

● We will review the Indicative Forestry Strategies produced under the 1990 guidance with a view to increasing their usefulness.

> **Glenlivet Estate**
>
> The 23,000 hectare estate at Glenlivet in Banffshire, owned by the Crown Estate, has long supported a community based upon upland farming activities. As well as farming and forestry, there is a large sporting interest covering grouse-shooting, salmon-fishing and deer-stalking which is let on a single sporting lease. In the late 1980s uncertainty about the future of hill and upland farming and the need to ensure that this remote rural area could continue to support a prosperous and settled community led to the Glenlivet Development Project whose aim was to encourage farm diversification and develop improved provision for tourists. Greater public access and the creation of new businesses have now achieved a strengthening of the base of the local economy.

SCOTLAND'S COAST

124 The Scottish coast is one of its most valuable assets. It has great variety and beauty; it provides a wide range of natural habitats of national and international importance; is extensively used for recreation and leisure; and it continues to have immense economic importance as a base for fishing, manufacturing, energy supply and transport. No part of Scotland is more than 65 kilometres from the coast. For rural areas, the coast is where the bulk of the population live and many rural businesses depend directly or indirectly on the resources that it has to offer.

Cattle Loch Indaal, Islay

"Scotland's Coast"

We will publish a discussion paper on coastal issues in early 1996 which will:

- Review Scotland's coastal heritage and the key developments and pressures affecting it.

- Review the policies and mechanisms in place for managing and controlling the developments and pressures.

- Set out proposals for improving present management, building on the successful approaches already being used in parts of Scotland based on the voluntary principle and partnership working.

125 The diversity of purposes that the coast serves leads inevitably to pressures on its resources and actual or potential conflicts between competing interests. Coastal areas are in demand for development related to the fishing industry, petrochemical industry, oil and gas extraction, waste and sewage disposal and transport. The coast provides the resources for fishing and aquaculture as well as small-scale activity such as cockle or seaweed harvesting. It is popular for tourism and this brings its own pressures for facilities and accommodation and the wear and tear of many people visiting the same area. These have an impact on the natural resources of the coast: its habitats and the wildlife that depends on them.

126 There are a number of ways in which these can be protected. Planning controls, legislation and special protection through nature conservation designations all play a part in this, as does better information and management of development pressures. Another valuable approach is the creation of local forums, such as those set up by Scottish Natural Heritage under its *Focus on Firths* initiative, where the various interests can get together to discuss how difficulties can be resolved and agree a way forward.

OUR HISTORY IN THE LAND

127 Scotland's countryside is rich in archaeological and historic remains; various sites, monuments, buildings and landscapes enable us to tell the story of the past from our present environment. The imprint these have left on the landscape is important to our sense of place and connects us to our roots. This is our common heritage and we all have a part to play in conserving it for the future.

Craw Stane, near Rhynie

Enjoying the Past

Remains of the past provide a source of enjoyment for us all, whether through informal recreation or through tourism initiatives. Historic Scotland cares for over 330 monuments which are open to visitors; and additional sites are in the care of such bodies as the National Trust for Scotland, the Forestry Commission and local authorities, while still others are in private ownership. We promote initiatives to manage and display buildings and monuments, such as Doors Open Day and support similar initiatives by others such as the Adopt-A-Monument Scheme run by the Council for Scottish Archaeology.

128 The evidence left by our ancestors can come under pressure from modern land-use and development, as well as from natural decay and we need to take care of it for the future. There are over 6000 scheduled ancient monuments and over 40,000 listed buildings in Scotland today. Grants are available from Historic Scotland towards the repair of our best historic buildings and the repair or management of monuments; some agricultural and forestry schemes also include provision for this.

129 The built heritage is a key part of today's landscape which belongs to us all. Relevant organisations have developed partnerships with each other as well as with local groups. Partnership enables a more integrated approach to Scotland's environment, as well as offering good value for money; amongst many examples are a new visitor centre at Callanish and the refurbishment of Duff House.

Duff House

130 Remnants of the past provide a source of employment in rural Scotland. The built heritage is a mainstay of the tourism industry, providing both direct employment and helping to extend the length of stay in rural areas. Monuments and buildings require ongoing care and maintenance and this provides work for local craftsmen and support for traditional building skills.

131 The diverse character of today's rural landscape is closely linked to its use by past generations. Conserving buildings in vernacular styles demands the winning of traditional building materials from local sources; this is of potentially greater benefit to the local economy than the importation of "lookalike" but physically unsuitable materials

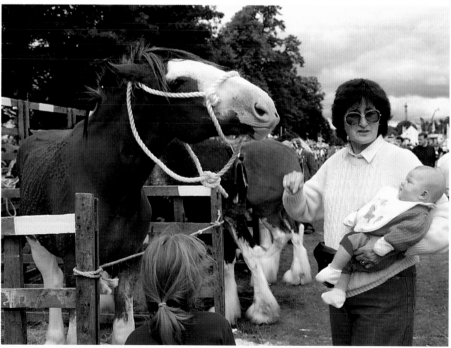

Perth Agricultural Show

from further afield. Only our own actions, for example respecting vernacular building styles or traditional forms of field boundaries, can ensure that our landscape will continue to tell us the story of our past.

Sustaining the Effort

132 We are determined to continue to protect and enhance our natural and built heritage and to take pride in Scotland's working landscapes. We intend to continue to move towards systems, such as cross-compliance, which deliver the full range of benefits to rural people and the population at large where the presumption will be that those who seek to use our countryside do so in ways which meet the wider objectives set out in this document. This is at the heart of sustainable development to which we are committed.

PROSPECTS FOR PROSPERITY

133   The economy of many parts of rural Scotland is thriving, its population continues to grow and there are good prospects for continued prosperity. The task of Government is to provide the framework within which we live, to open the path to opportunity and to safeguard those interests which cannot defend themselves. In all parts of Scotland this involves balancing the needs of the economy, the social and cultural structure of our communities and the needs of our environment. The characteristic of rural life which separates it from that of the town is the balance between these. In the rural community, the land is the dominant influence. It is not surprising therefore if the economic activities of rural communities have often been linked to traditional ways of life in agriculture, crofting, fishing and forestry. But now these activities provide the stage on which newer businesses are growing, like tourism, small scale manufacturing and fish farming.

Neil McKie repairing dyke, Dromore, Cairnsmore of Fleet

134   In this chapter we review the way in which rural Scotland is growing and the new markets and opportunities to which it has access and its increasing contribution to competitiveness in Scotland and the UK. Major support is given by Government to enabling rural communities to enjoy prosperous lives, through encouraging competition and enterprise, through providing the transport infrastructure and in working to enable the basic systems of rural Scotland, like agriculture, to flourish.

135   Rural areas are an integral part of the Scottish and wider economy. We cannot separate town and country, farmer and retiring incomer. The landscape of Scotland is the living reflection of many generations building successful communities on the natural resources which it provides, land and water, wind and rain, sea and sun; but above all people. These rural communities are the shapers and custodians of the land and they hold it for all of us, whether we go there as tourist, trader or to work.

Competitiveness

The Competitiveness White Paper set out in detail what the Government is doing to enhance the competitive position of the UK as a whole. Although improving competitiveness is primarily a matter for business itself, Government also has an important role. To facilitate enterprise and help business become internationally competitive, we shall continue to:

● create the framework in which companies can prosper – maintaining low inflation and sound public finances, making markets work more efficiently, removing unnecessary regulatory burdens, raising standards in education and training, and ensuring communication and transport infrastructure;

● help companies to help themselves – spreading best practice, sponsor business' needs, and where necessary, providing direct assistance, particularly for smaller firms, and investing in science and technology research.

The Success of Rural Areas

136 The 1995 White Paper on Competitiveness committed us to exploring how best to ensure that rural areas make an increasing contribution to competitiveness in Scotland and the UK. Many of the trends in employment and the rural economy were set out in *"Scottish Rural Life"*, published in the Rural Framework series in 1992. The impact of Europe was assessed in a further volume in the series entitled *"Pounds, Policies and Prospects"* published in association with Rural Forum, COSLA and Scottish Enterprise in 1993. Additional information set out in a form to assist the new councils assess their new responsibilities was published in *"The New Councils: Statistical Report"* published in 1995.

137 Improving competitiveness applies just as much to businesses in rural areas as to those in our towns and cities. Without successful, competitive, businesses it will be impossible to achieve self-sustaining prosperity. The most recent trends show rural Scotland to be performing well as judged by many of the key economic indicators. Rural Scotland is diverse and each area has its own characteristics and needs. The signs are that rural Scotland has adapted well to structural changes and is now well placed to continue to generate the jobs and the incomes that will be needed for a prosperous future.

138 The population of most rural areas continues to rise, a process which began in the 1970s after 50 years of decline. Overall, the population of rural

First Results from Scottish Rural Life 2

● Unemployment in rural Scotland in 1994 was, at 8.4% still lower than in urban Scotland and there are considerable variations within districts.

● Seasonal employment remains a problem in those areas dependent on tourist-related activity.

● Prices tend to be higher in rural Scotland and earnings lower.

● Self employment is important in agriculture, fishing, tourism, leisure and textiles and many people hold a variety of part-time jobs.

● Despite large reductions in agricultural employment, primary sector activities are still regarded as mainstays of the rural economy.

● Losses in agricultural employment have been more than matched by increases in service sector employment.

● Long term unemployment tends to be less severe in rural Scotland and rates for this group have fallen.

● Twice as many people, proportionately, work at home in rural Scotland, reaching some 21% in Stewartry and Orkney.

● Information on recipients of income support and housing benefit suggest that the proportion of claimants is less in rural Scotland than in Scotland as a whole.

● House prices are now more favourable compared to those of towns.

Scotland increased by 3.2% over the period 1981-91, compared with a decline of 1.4% in Scotland as a whole. Rising population suggests economic success. An important measure of economic success is, of course, employment and in rural areas employment levels have risen in recent years. There has been a growth of 6.5% in employment in rural Scotland 1981-91 compared with a 1.1% growth in Scotland as a whole. The change has varied by area, but employment rose in 25 out of the 31 rural local authority districts over this period.

Population and Employment Change in Rural Scotland   1981-91

District	Population Change (%)	Employment Change (%)
Angus	2.4	3.1
Annandale and Eskdale	4.2	8.6
Argyll and Bute	0.8	2.5
Badenoch and Strathspey	11.4	10.3
Banff and Buchan	3.4	12.0
Berwickshire	4.2	21.5
Caithness	-3.4	-3.2
Clydesdale	1.5	4.1
Cumnock and Doon Valley	-4.4	-27.9
Ettrick and Lauderdale	3.2	1.4
Gordon	20.9	40.7
Inverness	9.4	8.8
Kincardine and Deeside	26.9	57.3
Kyle and Carrick	0.3	1.2
Lochaber	-0.9	4.3
Moray	0.9	10.6
Nairn	6.6	72.5
Nithsdale	0.7	5
North East Fife	7.5	5.6
Orkney	2.0	13.2
Perth and Kinross	4.7	4.0
Ross and Cromarty	4.6	6.8
Roxburgh	0.0	1.3
Shetland	-14.5	-3.7
Skye and Lochalsh	10.5	77.2
Stewartry	2.9	-7.1
Stirling	1.5	3.7
Sutherland	-1.1	13.2
Tweeddale	7.0	-3.4
Western Isles	-6.8	18.6
Wigtown	-1.0	-16.9
Rural Scotland	**3.5**	**6.5**
Scotland	**-1.4**	**1.1**

Source: Census of Population 1981 and 1991

GRO for Scotland

Department of Employment

Census of Employment 1981 and 1991

Population and Employment

139 The structure of employment in rural areas is now much closer to that of Scotland as a whole and rural Scotland has fared better than the rest of the country during a period of changing industrial structure from the early 1980s. There has been a dramatic rise in service sector employment which has more than offset the decline in the more traditional industries in the primary and manufacturing sectors. Even so, primary industries still remain important in many rural areas, with agriculture, forestry and fishing accounting for 4.4% of rural employment.

Employment by Industrial Sector

	Scotland 1991 %	% Change 1981-91	Rural Scotland 1991 %	% Change 1981-91
Primary	4.3	-26.5	5.8	-40.00
Manufacturing	19.0	-24.1	17.3	-8.5
Construction	6.5	-6.8	7.1	4.1
Services	70.2	14.	69.8	19.2
Overall Change		0.7		6.5

Source: Census of Employment 1981 and 1991

140 It is service industries not traditionally associated with rural areas that are growing the most. Both tourism and retailing figure highly but the main changes have come from increased employment in schools, hospitals and social services. Rural Scotland also has many people who are self employed in industries such as agriculture, fishing, textiles (like Harris Tweed weavers) and hotels. In many rural areas people can often have a variety of part time jobs.

Employment Increases in Rural Scotland by Industry 1981-91

Industry	Total Employment 1991	Increase %
Education	43,009	55.0
Medical/Other health: veterinary services	45,620	37.1
Other Services to the general public	22,802	62.6
Retail Distribution	57,911	15.7
Hotels and Catering	45,062	17.6
Business Services	14,832	61.7

Source: Census of Employment 1981 and 1991

Responding to Change

141 Today the average rural unemployment rate is below the national average, as it has been in the past. Together with the encouraging growth in jobs, this points to a rural workforce that has adapted well to changes in the labour market over the last ten years.

142 Growth in the overall levels of rural population and employment suggest economic success, a marked change from the downward trend in both indicators for many decades during the last century. Moreover, the position varies quite markedly across the constituent parts of rural Scotland and this makes any broad generalisation on rural economic performance difficult. Rural districts near the more successful urban areas, particularly those near Aberdeen, are doing especially well while more remote areas, particularly the islands, have more progress to make. Improvements in transport infrastructure have greatly reduced travel times, especially by road, and technological improvements have enabled businesses dependent on modern communications to locate in more remote rural areas. Thus rural Scotland contains a diverse mixture of areas in which the challenge is to build prosperity more evenly across rural Scotland, across business sectors and among different groups of the population.

Rural Business Units

It has been suggested that commercial activities associated with a rural estate whose predominant activity is husbandry should be assessed as a single trading unit for income tax, capital gains tax and inheritance tax purposes. Under this concept of a Rural Business Unit, income from commercial activities traditionally associated with a rural estate, together with evolving diversified activities, would be treated as trading income. Relevant activities would be eligible for business property relief from inheritance tax and from capital gains tax reliefs. We are considering this case.

Tree extraction, Torridon

Encouraging Enterprise

143 The principal vehicles for the encouragement of economic activity in rural areas are the enterprise networks of 22 local enterprise companies covering the whole of Scotland. From the point of view of rural communities, the key aspect of local enterprise companies is their local character. Although, as a network, they have the powers, skills and financial muscle of a national development agency, they are individually able to respond to local needs in a flexible and responsive way and to deliver individually tailored packages of economic development, environmental improvement and training services to match the varying economic needs of rural areas.

144 The local enterprise companies, and their parent bodies Scottish Enterprise and Highlands and Islands Enterprise, work in partnership with other bodies, agencies and local government to encourage the involvement of all parts of the community in the task of economic regeneration. The achievements of the Cowal Initiative, the Rural Stirling Partnership, the

Angus Glens Initiative and many similar ventures involving the local enterprise companies demonstrate that a commitment to this partnership approach is a critical factor in achieving success.

The Cowal Initiative

In 1992, the United States Navy service base on the Holy Loch was closed. For the previous 30 years, it had dominated the economy of Dunoon and the Cowal peninsula. The response to the base closure was a three year initiative led by Argyll and the Islands Enterprise, in partnership with the Cowal Enterprise Trust, Highlands and Islands Enterprise, Argyll and Bute District Council, Bute and Cowal Tourist Board, Cowal Community Councils Platform, Dunoon Chamber of Commerce and Strathclyde Regional Council.

The initiative, which included expenditure on finance for business, environmental improvements, training and community development, proved highly successful and an independent evaluation concluded in February 1995 that:

● by the end of 1994, more than 730 additional jobs had been created or retained, with the figure forecast to reach 950 by 1997, thus replacing the jobs lost as a result of the base closure

● the initiative had successfully attracted inward investment and diversified the economic base

● the initiative had been successful in its economic impact and that confidence had been instilled in the community

● the initiative had proved that a well-resourced and locally focused organisation can deliver positive benefits in the regeneration and economic development of rural areas.

Planning Careers

The Scottish Office is planning a conference on the issues and problems facing rural careers offices in Scotland. Transport problems and the lack of local employment and training opportunities pose unique challenges for the careers service and its clients. High quality, appropriate and informative careers guidance is crucial if young people are to make the best career decisions. A conference involving careers service staff from rural areas, local enterprise companies and others will offer the opportunity to share good practice, to identify and address problem areas and explore possible solutions.

145 From this established basis of local decision making and partnership with others, the Enterprise networks will continue to promote the development of rural areas. For example, targets for Highlands and Islands Enterprise in 1995-96 include:

● **creation or retention of 3,400 direct jobs;**

● **creation or retention of 900 indirect jobs;**

● **555 businesses committed to achieving _Investors in People_;**

● **a continuing increase in the proportion of trainees achieving a recognised qualification.**

This is in a primarily rural area where a long term trend of population and employment decline has been reversed.

146 Many of the development opportunities in rural areas arise from the quality of the environment. The Enterprise networks have powers to promote and support environmental renewal which can be instrumental in preserving and strengthening this source of

competitive advantage. Scottish Enterprise, Highlands & Islands Enterprise and their networks of local enterprise companies are also in a position to ensure that opportunities are exploited in a way which is sensitive to the local environment and that the economic development generated is sustainable.

Backing Winners

147 While the enterprise networks offer the primary route for encouraging economic development, other bodies have an important role to play. Local authorities have their own functions in economic development, as well as being the principal providers of supporting infrastructure. National agencies, such as Scottish Homes, Scottish National Heritage, and now the Scottish Environmental Protection Agency also have an important role to play. Given the importance of tourism in rural areas, the Scottish Tourist Board and the area tourist boards have much to contribute to that industry. The European Structural Funds also play an important part in the financial underpinning of public sector development and training. Finally, and perhaps most importantly, the voluntary sector, including such bodies as enterprise trusts, is a significant means of delivering some of the services of local enterprise companies. The local enterprise companies and their parent bodies, Scottish Enterprise and Highlands and Islands Enterprise, work in partnership with other parts of the public, private and voluntary sectors to encourage the involvement of the whole community in the task of economic regeneration.

Driving sheep, Cairnsmore of Fleet

148 There are many examples which show how economic development in rural areas has been stimulated by the enterprise networks, operating in co-operation with the private sector; and demonstrating that the economic potential of rural areas extends beyond traditional industries and traditional methods of working.

The Wise Group and Rosswise

The Wise Group has developed an innovative and successful approach which combines high quality training for the unemployed with the provision of environmental and social services. The Group has mainly operated in and around Glasgow, but has also undertaken projects in Newham, in London and in Lanarkshire. Recently, the model used by the Wise Group has been adapted for use in a rural area under a franchise arrangement, through the establishment of *Rosswise* in the Ross and Cromarty area. *Rosswise* uses the same principles as the Wise Group, that an intermediate labour market can be created by combining high quality training with experience on practical projects which provide social and environmental services such as home insulation for the elderly, footpath work and the improvement of play areas.

BT Network in the Highlands and Islands

Teleworking and Out-sourcing

149 In 1989, Highlands and Islands Enterprise joined British Telecommunications plc in a major collaboration to bring state of the art telecommunications facilities to all parts of the Highlands and Islands area, in the forefront of the United Kingdom installation programme. Highlands and Islands Enterprise contributed £5 million to a £20 million investment. The telecommunications infrastructure of the area is now based an integrated services digital network providing high speed and high integrity digital data communications services, together with computer facilities which provide an access network for local, national and international services at local call rates.

150 This has encouraged the establishment of a range of jobs based on information technology. BT itself has established a computer help desk at Thurso, employing more than 70 people to provide a range of telephone services to subscribers throughout the United Kingdom. Similarly, Hoskyns has a business process out-sourcing centre, which will eventually employ 200 people to undertake administrative operations (such as council tax claims or parking fines) for distant local authorities. The underlying principle is that modern information technology and telecommunications have removed the need for many contemporary office operations to be undertaken in conventional urban locations. Business process re-engineering and electronic work flow techniques enable complex and discretionary tasks to be handled through distributed networks. This opens up an exciting range of options, from individual home-working, to directly managed local work centres, to remotely located facilities managed by contract suppliers of administrative services.

151 The distinctive circumstances of the Highlands and Islands, where less than 7% of Scotland's population live in an area covering half her land mass, means that Highlands & Islands Enterprise has additional powers to assist social development projects which help maintain and enhance rural communities. In 1994-95, Highlands & Islands Enterprise supported over 300 such projects through Community Action Grants. The projects include support for a wide range of cultural activities as well as the development of community facilities, such as swimming pools, sports clubs and village halls. As with its other activities, Highlands & Islands Enterprise gives the highest priority to fragile, remote areas. It is the capacity to combine this kind of support with assistance to employment creating business projects and support for access to modern telecommunications infrastructure which has enabled Highlands & Islands Enterprise to promote the advantages of modern technology and traditional values in support of its rural areas.

Future Prospects

152 Economic development in rural areas requires determination. But many modern trends are working in favour of rural areas, for example, improved electronic communications and an ever-increasing demand for a good quality environment and a high quality of life. We believe that the support networks are in place to ensure that continued progress can be made in identifying suitable economic opportunities and in taking advantage of those opportunities. The traditional rural industries of fishing, forestry, agriculture and agricultural products will remain important in many Scottish rural communities but there are also many examples which demonstrate the scope for diversifying the economic base of rural areas.

Tweed Horizons Centre for Sustainable Technology

The Tweed Horizons project which began in 1993 used the former St Columba's College in Newtown St Boswells to provide accommodation for businesses and seminars related to sustainable development and the provision of support to new and existing businesses in this area of development. The project is being taken forward by Scottish Borders Enterprise and has a total cost of £2.7 million from June 1993 to March 1997. Over 500 metres of office and laboratory space has already been provided and 12 separate companies have already been attracted to the project, creating employment for 39 people. In addition, an integrated land-use plan has been developed for the 10 hectares surrounding the building, including a forest garden, a native nursery, a composting trial and organic horticulture. The building will be powered and heated by a specially developed biofuel generator.

The companies attracted to the *Tweed Horizons* banner are all associated with various forms of sustainable development, frequently involving the use of advanced technology. They include companies in:

- sophisticated energy management, as well as providing advice on a range of energy matters, undertakes a complete design, supply and fit service for combined heat and power plants

- developing rural land based projects into sustainable businesses, including the farming of fungi, tree nurseries and the recycling of organic waste

- developing markets for a tyre re-cycling system and reclaimed products of gas, oil, carbon and steel

- design and manufacture of odour control systems based on activated carbon and bio-filtration

- design and patenting of components for advanced bicycles;

- design and patenting of clothing to enhance the human thermo-regulatory system, based on research into adipose tissue;

- the use of wood for power generation which has set up a producer group for growing willow coppice (for fuel) on agricultural set-aside land.

LIVING OFF THE LAND

153 Rural Scotland is built on its traditional industries: agriculture and crofting, fishing and forestry. These shape the land and provide the foundation for other businesses like tourism and fish-farming which are of vital economic importance. But while the new industries excite attention we cannot neglect the role of the features of rural life which have shaped our countryside, and without which we will not be able to attract new investment.

Harvesting

SCOTTISH AGRICULTURE

154 For many people, agriculture is rural Scotland. Some three-quarters of Scotland's total land area is agricultural, with 86% of that classified as Less Favoured Areas of which the majority is hill and upland grazing suitable only for sheep and cattle breeding and rearing. On average, Scottish farms are much larger in area than elsewhere in the United Kingdom or the rest of the European Community. In the Highlands and

Average Farm Size	
Country	Area, hectares
Scotland	123
United Kingdom	77
European Union	14

Islands there are also many relatively small crofts which are farmed on a part-time basis, but which form the core of rural communities and are invaluable in conserving outstanding wildlife habitats.

The Importance of Scottish Agriculture

● The annual gross output of agriculture is around £1,800 million. This generates aggregate income to farmers and their families of around £450 million.

● Livestock and livestock products account for 70% of output; arable accounts for most of the remainder.

● Some 68,000 people are engaged in agriculture; slightly less than half are occupiers (self-employed) and the remainder employees or family labour. Agriculture supports over 200,00 people in a variety of related industries.

● In the Highlands and Islands some 10% of the work force is involved in agriculture.

● Some 65% of farms are owner occupied with an average net wealth estimated at some £350,000; tenanted farms account for the remainder with an average net wealth of almost £150,000.

The Common Agricultural Policy

155 The Common Agricultural Policy was undoubtedly successful in achieving its initial goal of eliminating post-war food shortages and making the European Community more self-sufficient in food production terms. These successes must, however, be set against the high cost of the policy, much of which is attributable to the fact that it has stimulated food production well beyond what would have been accomplished by market forces on their own. The need to address the problems created by this overproduction has led to a series of measures being introduced to eliminate surpluses, limit production, reduce costs and protect the environment.

The Objectives of Agricultural Policy

The Common Agricultural Policy has had a major impact on UK agricultural policy since the UK joined the European Community in 1973 and the Government seeks to ensure that the development of European Community policies has due regard to the needs and circumstances of Scottish farmers and crofters. The Government's main policy objectives for Scottish agriculture within the CAP are:

● to improve the competitive efficiency of agriculture in Scotland and assist its adjustment to changing market conditions

● to ensure a proper balance between agriculture and other rural development interests including conservation of the environment

● to maintain and develop assistance for those farming and crofting in marginal conditions

156 The most significant changes were introduced under the 1992 CAP Reform mechanisms through reduced price support, compensated for by livestock headage and area based support which in turn was limited by supply controls such as quotas and set-aside. Most significantly, the 1992 reforms introduced agri-environment measures into the CAP for the first time.

157 While there is general agreement that Scottish farmers have fared well since 1992, Government policy is to pursue further changes in the CAP to create a more efficient and competitive farming industry capable of providing high quality produce while at the same time protecting and enhancing the environment. To achieve this and to cut the cost of the CAP to the taxpayer and the consumer, the Government will continue to press for progressive reductions in production-related support and targeting for remaining support more effectively on the social and economic needs of rural communities, particularly those which are most disadvantaged. There is also a desire to reduce the bureaucracy associated especially with supply controls and reduce the burden of form-filling which is placed upon farmers.

158 The goal of safeguarding and enhancing the rural environment should be at the heart of a reformed CAP, with policy mechanisms geared towards specific objectives. Progressive reductions in production-related support can be

expected to yield large savings. Whilst it should not be assumed that all savings would automatically be available to farming or that action at EC level would always be the best way to approach environmental objectives, a substantial level of public funding to secure environmental benefits would be justified.

159 In addition to these internal pressures for change, there will also be external pressures which are likely to influence future CAP policy. One such pressure is the possible enlargement of the European Union which would place an unbearable strain on the Common Agricultural Policy as it is presently organised. The GATT agreement and subsequent further GATT negotiations towards the turn of the century will also bring change. It is important that these issues are addressed by the European Union over the next few years with environmental considerations occupying a prominent position on what will be a wide-ranging agenda.

Support to Agriculture

160 Direct payments to farmers and crofters are made through a variety of schemes, some of which are wholly financed by the European Community, some wholly financed by the United Kingdom, and others funded from both sources. In addition to direct subsidies, Scottish producers also benefit from a range of other indirect support measures under the Common Agricultural Policy which affect market prices and therefore incomes. These include intervention buying (triggered for certain products when prices fall below specified levels); the imposition of levies, in order to prevent cheap food imports undercutting Community produce; and export subsidies which allow home-grown produce to be sold at a competitive price outside the Community.

The Government Commitment to Agriculture

- Direct subsidy expenditure on Scottish agriculture in 1994 is estimated at £332 million - approaching 75% of the estimated income to farmers and their families. The expectation is that direct subsidies in 1995 could be around £400 million.

- Indirect subsidies in the form of higher prices due to import tariffs, intervention buying and quota arrangements are also significant. Estimates of this vary but could be of the same order as the direct subsidy figure.

- In the remotest rural areas hill sheep farming predominates. On average, direct subsidies to hill sheep farms in less favoured areas account for more than double the income to the farmer and spouse.

- Even on cereal farms the subsidy support is substantial and has increased significantly in recent years. On average direct subsidies account for one and a quarter times the income to the farmer and spouse.

- Apart from the spending generated by these subsidised incomes, the support maintains agricultural output and employment in rural areas at levels well above those that would obtain if there was no support.

- It is estimated that the loss of 1000 jobs in agriculture would result in the loss of 1,442 jobs in firms which supply goods and services to agriculture, and a loss of a further 441 jobs due to the resulting reduction in consumer spending.

Agricultural Support: The Main Schemes

Hill Livestock Compensatory Allowances support hill farmers in the Less Favoured Areas and are graded according to the severity of the natural handicap. Under the 1994 scheme payments are expected to total almost £41 million (£23 million for cattle, over £17 million for sheep).

Sheep Annual Premium is the largest livestock subsidy scheme in Scotland. It is paid on ewes and helps to compensate sheepmeat producers for loss of income when the market price falls below the European Community reference price. Payments made under the 1994 scheme are estimated at over £90 million.

Suckler Cow Premium is the main support for production from the beef herd. Following CAP Reform payments increased to £51 million in 1994 and will reach about £65 million in 1995.

Beef Special Premium: payments under the 1994 scheme amounted to £31 million and will rise to over £35 million in the 1995 scheme.

Arable Area Payments make payments for arable crops to compensate for reductions in indirect support which in 1994 amounted to £117 million.

Our Commitment to Service

161 The Scottish Office published in 1993 the Charter Standard Statement *"Serving Scottish Farmers"* (and updated it in a second edition in 1995). It set out aims for the provision of a high quality service to farmers and listed over 25 targets relating mainly to the processing of applications and claims for grants and subsidies. Again in 1993, The Scottish Office, in conjunction with the Crofters Commission, published a Charter Standard Statement *"Serving Crofting"* for crofters. The Scottish Office publishes each year information on the extent to which it achieves its targets. In 1993-94, most targets were achieved to the extent of 90% or better.

162 The Government also provides substantial support to agriculture through research, development, education and advisory services. £71 million will be spent on these services in 1995-96, of which some £40 million relates to research. The *"Policy for Science and Technology"* reaffirms the Government's commitment to support all aspects of agricultural science, including non-medical biology, physical science and mathematics; research into productivity; land use and related environmental, economic and social consequences; and research on food and its nutritional effects on animals and humans where that has implications for agriculture.

Selling The Quality Scottish Product

163 Some two-thirds of the output of the Scottish food and drink industry (excluding whisky and other alcoholic drinks) is sold outside Scotland, a substantial part of it outside the United Kingdom. Recognising the increasing challenges and opportunities for Scottish agriculture in this highly competitive market at home and abroad, the Government have introduced a range of measures to encourage food marketing strategies. The food industry in Scotland has made good use of the incentives for investment available through processing and marketing grants from the European Community to strengthen its market position and develop new products. Support is also available through grants to producer groups and others under the Marketing Development Scheme.

164 In 1993, the Government set up the Scottish Food Strategy Group to identify opportunities for the Scottish food and drink industry, particularly with regard to exporting. Support for food exporters comes from the enterprise network and *Food from Britain* among others. Food exporters will benefit from improved co-ordination of export support as a result of the Export Strategy for Scotland, which is led by Scottish Trade International and has the support of all the key export support agencies in Scotland.

165 One of Scotland's advantages in marketing its produce is its reputation for an unspoilt natural environment and high quality husbandry. The major retail outlets are placing increased emphasis on quality products in response to consumer demand. *Scottish Quality Farm Assurance*, developed by the National Farmers' Union in Scotland with support from the Government, has an important role to play. A number of quality schemes for Scottish farmed produce have been established in recent years and the new Scottish Food Quality Certification Ltd will provide a focus for future developments.

Scottish Potatoes

The marketing of potatoes, an important cash crop for many Scottish farmers, is currently controlled by the Potato Marketing Scheme administered by the Potato Marketing Board. The Scheme will end in 1997. The Board is preparing proposals for a successor body and there will be particular Scottish interest in arrangements for the seed potato sector. Scottish seed potatoes are renowned for their high health status and quality which is backed up by a classification scheme administered by The Scottish Office. Scotland has around 600 seed potato growers, producing some 400,000 tonnes annually, with a value of £30 million.

Lagavulin distillery

Whisky

Scotch whisky is Scotland's second and the United Kingdom's fifth largest export earning industry. The value of the export earnings from whisky has been rising steadily over the past 20 years and in 1994 exceeded £2,100 million. Following rationalisations in the mid 1980's the level of employment within the industry has stabilised at around 14,500. Distilling is not a labour intensive process and accounts for only 20% of the work force. The bulk of the work force in the industry is in the blending and bottling plants concentrated in the central belt of Scotland . There are, however, especially strong links between the whisky industry and other industries such as agriculture, glass-making, packaging, transport, wholesale and retail sales, and tourism. There are also strong intra-industry links because distillers sell or swap output for blending. The strong backward linkages give the sector a high employment multiplier effect. The Scotch whisky industry is a keystone of Scotland's economic structure and of great significance to its rural economies.

Scottish Milk

Important changes in milk marketing followed the deregulation of the marketing of milk by dairy farmers. The Government brought forward legislation enabling the three Milk Marketing Boards to submit reorganisation schemes which would revoke the statutory schemes and replace the statutory boards with voluntary arrangements. Most dairy farmers joined the milk co-operatives set up to succeed the milk marketing boards, but many did not and now sell direct to processor companies. Deregulation of the milk market has allowed normal market forces to operate, subject to milk quotas and has, for the first time, introduced genuine competition to the dairy sector, benefiting consumers and the industry.

Developing Scottish Agriculture

166 Scotland's farmers and crofters have benefited from a range of development programmes over the past decade. The Integrated Development Programme for the Western Isles and the Agricultural Development Programme for the Scottish Islands (excluding the Western Isles) contributed nearly £60 million to farming and crofting, while the Rural Enterprise Programme for the Highlands and Islands offered support of more than £14 million for economic diversification. Almost all of Scotland's rural areas are now covered by designations under Objectives 1 and 5b of the European Commission Structural Funds and this will mean substantial extra support for economic development in Scotland's most fragile rural areas.

The Highlands and Islands Agricultural Programme: Objective 1

167 The Highlands and Islands Agricultural Programme is part of the £260 million Objective 1 Programme for the area which is being funded by the Government and the European Commission. Over the 6 year period of Objective 1 designation the Programme will provide over £23 million additional funds to farmers and crofters in the area. The Programme has three separate schemes designed to meet the special needs of farmers and crofters in the Highlands and Islands:

- *Agricultural Business Improvement* is administered by The Scottish Office and provides assistance towards a wide range of capital projects, and agricultural and environmental improvements. Investment and training priorities are identified in resource audits undertaken by independent consultants which form the basis of applications for grant assistance. Over £18.5 million will be spent over the duration of the Scheme.

- *Marketing* provides assistance to farmers and crofters to market existing products and rural services, and to develop new ones. The Scheme can help with promotional material, trade exhibitions, feasibility studies and product development as well as general marketing. The Scheme is administered by Highlands and Islands Enterprise, via the LEC network, on behalf of The Scottish Office . Expenditure will be around £3 million over the duration of the Scheme.

- *Crofting Township Development* encourages community projects in crofting townships by providing incentives based on development plans produced by the crofters themselves. The range of projects which can feature in development plans is potentially very wide. The Scheme is administered by the Crofters Commission on behalf of The Scottish Office , and around £1.5 million will be available over the life of the Scheme.

168 The Scottish Office provides reports to the local partnership which oversees the progress of the Objective 1 Programme. The level of interest in the Programme and the uptake of grants suggests that it will be a major success.

Diversifying Scottish Agriculture: Objective 5b

169 Farmers and crofters are increasingly recognising the need to diversify into activities other than agriculture and to explore the opportunities for both new agricultural products and the use of conventional crops for non-

Mist and hills, Wolfhill

food purposes. Government support for diversification was available through the Rural Enterprise Programme in the Highlands and Islands and will form the basis for the new Objective 5b Agricultural Diversification Programmes.

170 Four of Scotland's rural areas have been designated under Objective 5b by the European Commission: Borders, Dumfries and Galloway, North and West Grampian, and Rural Stirling and Upland Tayside. Agriculture contributes considerably to the economy and employment in all of these areas, but the Government and the European Commission wish to assist farmers to widen their economic bases by encouraging activities which will provide income from non-agricultural sources.

171 The local development plans (known as Single Programme Documents) for all four Objective 5b areas include measures to encourage agricultural diversification. Following a wide-ranging consultation exercise, The Scottish Office is preparing detailed diversification programmes which will provide around £10 million in Government and European Commission funds to farmers in the Objective 5b areas. Subject to approval of these programmes by local partnerships (and Parliamentary approval of enabling legislation), it is proposed to provide assistance towards a wide range of innovative and exciting projects. For example, farmers in the four Objective 5b areas could receive assistance to grow crops for pharmaceutical purposes or alternative energy sources as well as moving into high added value produce, such as mushrooms. Alternative livestock breeding and rearing, for example fibre-producing goats, rabbits, shellfish and snails, are also eligible for assistance.

The Scottish Agricultural College

172 Educational support is provided through the Scottish Agricultural College which offers a wide range of courses to its 1,200 students, covering agriculture, horticulture, land use, food handling and hygiene. Funding for educational support through grant-in-aid in 1995-96 to £7.3 million. The College also receives financial support for providing advisory services to

farmers through its network of field advisers who are located throughout Scotland. Grant-in-aid to the advisory services in 1995-96 is £6.4 million, and farmers are charged for some services.

The Future for Scottish Agriculture

173 Increased farm incomes and direct payments to farmers in recent years have put Scottish agriculture in a good position to face the challenges and opportunities of a more competitive market place in the future. We believe that, against the background of the development of the Common Agricultural Policy and GATT, progress will increasingly depend on the ability of farmers and food processors to meet the needs of the consumer with lower levels of public support. Scotland's reputation for high quality husbandry and produce, based on an attractive and unspoilt natural environment, is a powerful marketing advantage on which Scottish farmers can build. We are committed to providing a framework within which agriculture can compete and wider rural development and environmental objectives be achieved.

Farm and Crofter Forestry

Woodlands on farms and croft land can provide an additional source of income for those directly involved and conservation benefits for the community at large. The Government has sought to encourage farmers and crofters by:

- Providing financial assistance, in the form of annual payments, to take land out of agricultural production and convert it to woodland through the *Farm Woodland Premium Scheme*. These payments are in addition to the planting grants available through the Forestry Commission *Woodland Grant Scheme* and in just over 3 years since the Scheme was launched some 1,000 applications have been approved representing over 15,000 hectares of new woodlands.

- Supporting legislation, the Crofters Forestry (Scotland) Act 1991 which provided for crofters' common grazings committees to plant woodland on the common grazings subject to the approval of the landlord and the Crofters Commission and thereby permitting them to benefit from forestry grants.

- Providing financial assistance to farmers in Environmentally Sensitive Areas to exclude stock from areas of semi-natural woodland to encourage regeneration.

- Negotiating a change in the rules of the Arable Area Payments Scheme which allows farmers to count arable land entered into the Woodland Grant and Farm Woodland Premium Schemes towards their set-aside obligations.

CROFTING

174 Crofting offers a distinctive culture and way of life and has played an important role in helping to retain population in the remoter, rural areas of Scotland. The Government continues to help strengthen and support crofting communities by providing:

Achriesgill, near Kinlochbervie

- **funding for the work of the Crofters Commission, responsible for the administration and development of crofting and with a duty to keep under review all matters relating to crofting;**

- **assistance for the construction and improvement of croft houses;**

- **grants for agricultural improvements;**

- **livestock improvement schemes designed to help crofting townships improve the quality of their sheep and cattle;**

- **grants to veterinary practices in the Highlands and Islands to ensure that veterinary services are available at a standard charge regardless of physical remoteness.**

In 1994-95, approximately £10 million was spent on support for crofting.

Crofting Trusts

175 Crofting trusts are a form of land ownership which provide a means of transferring power and responsibility to local communities in the Highlands and Islands of Scotland. The individual crofters retain all their rights under the Crofting Acts, including the right to buy their individual crofts, if they so wish, whilst the crofting trust provides a framework for ensuring good management for the townships in question and for exploiting development opportunities. The crofting trust concept has been pioneered recently in Assynt and Borve and Annishadder in Skye, although the Stornoway Trust provides a long-standing example of a more broadly based form of community ownership.

176 In the early part of the century, the Government acquired large areas of land to create new crofting townships and there are currently approximately 1,400 croft holdings owned by the Secretary of State extending to over 100,000 hectares. The Government is interested in exploring the possibility of transferring the ownership of this land to crofting trusts providing there is sufficient interest and support at the local

Crofter Housing

Croft houses form a significant part of the housing stock in the Highlands and Islands and, in the past, crofters have experienced poor housing conditions. The Crofters Building Grants and Loans Scheme provides grant assistance and low cost loans for the construction of new and the improvement of existing croft houses. In 1994-95, the Government spent almost £5 million on this support and, in total some 7,000 new houses have been built and more than 10,000 improvements made since the scheme began in 1912, with obvious benefits to the crofting community.

Croft Entrant Scheme

The Lochaber and Argyll Croft Entrant Scheme is a recent initiative launched by the Crofters Commission in partnership with local enterprise companies. It is designed to help to retain young people in crofting communities by encouraging elderly, inactive or absentee crofters to release their land to new, young entrants.

Forestry Policy

The Government's forestry policies are based on a steady expansion of tree cover, to increase the many benefits which woodlands provide, and the sustainable management of existing woods and forests. We encourage:

● sustainable, multiple purpose forestry

● safeguarding of ancient semi-natural woodlands

● enhancing the contribution of all forests to the economy and the environment

● creating a variety of woodlands and forests, including native woodlands, community woodland and farm woodlands as well as larger forests primarily to increase the supply of timber for industry.

level. We will be issuing a consultation paper seeking views on the scope for further crofting trusts both on The Scottish Office crofting estates and on crofting land currently in private ownership.

FORESTRY

177 A policy of forestry expansion over the last seventy-five years has resulted in the doubling of creation of Scotland's forest and woodland cover, which is now about 1.2 million hectares, 15% of land area. There are about 122,000 hectares of semi natural remnants of ancient woodland - 16,000 hectares of pinewoods and 106,000 hectares broadleaved woodlands.

178 Forestry supports some 10,500 jobs in Scotland in forest management, timber harvesting and haulage and wood processing. In 1994 Scotland's forests and woodlands produced just over 3 million cubic metres of timber, nearly all of it softwood from forests planted twenty five and more years ago. The timber harvest has risen by 250% over the last twenty years. This increase has fed major new investment in timber processing in Scotland, for example Caledonian Paper at Irvine and Norbord Highland at Inverness. About three-quarters of the timber currently produced in Scotland is processed in Scotland. The timber harvest from existing forests and woodlands is set to increase to 8 million cubic metres over the next twenty years providing opportunities for further investment and employment in harvesting and wood processing.

Scots pine

Native woodlands

179 Scotland's native woodlands contribute greatly to the diversity of the countryside. However they are only a remnant of what was once an extensive range of habitats. Their rich bryophyte communities and mixtures of woodland species reflect Scotland's oceanic climate, giving them an international importance. But many are unmanaged and unprotected, making little economic contribution to their locality and unable to regenerate because of grazing. In recent years a number of partnerships have been established to sustain and expand native woodland habitats. They include Scottish Native Woods, Highland Birchwoods, The Caledonian Partnership, Tayside Native Woodlands Initiative and the Northwest Sutherland Native Woodland Initiative. We are assessing the achievements of woodland initiatives throughout Britain, to identify best practices and promote them more widely.

Highland Birchwoods

Highland Birchwoods is a charitable company jointly funded by the Forestry Commission, Highlands and Islands Enterprise, Highland Regional Council and Scottish Natural Heritage, which through three full-time advisors aims to encourage woodland management by increasing the commercial return to woodland owners. Recent examples of successful projects include:

● the cultivation of shiitake mushrooms on small roundwood which would otherwise have had little value. Commercial cropping of culinary mushrooms is expected to begin in 1996

● the introduction of manufacturing methods to make flooring from timber that otherwise would have been used for firewood.

Through Highland Birchwoods over 650 hectares of woodland have been entered into the Woodland Grant Scheme and a further 1,600 hectares is in prospect, ensuring that future management will be based on sound, sustainable principles.

180 The woodland environment is ideally suited to a wide range of recreational pursuits. Income can be generated with little additional investment in forest infrastructure. As well as providing additional income to the forest unit, recreation facilities can enhance the visitor attractiveness of a locality and contribute in that way to the local economy. The Forestry Commission is developing a recreation best practice pack for woodland owners including advice on how to make the most of opportunities and where to go for help.

Forests to Sustain Local Communities

181 There is a growing interest in increasing community participation in forestry as a means of providing social and economic benefits to people in rural areas. *The Forests and People in Rural Areas Initiative* (FAPIRA), an informal partnership of Government and non-Government organisations is exploring opportunities for increasing community participation in forestry. It has published a discussion document with a view to stimulating debate on the role which forests and forestry can play in sustainable rural development and is planning to hold a conference in the spring of 1996.

Native Woods Management

The Forestry Commission will build on its partnerships within a wider programme to encourage management of native woods, including the establishment of a broadleaved marketing development group to help woodland owners realise the economic potential of their woods. The aim is to:

● encourage sustainable management of these woods,

● secure their future

● ensure that training, advice, information and opportunities for collaboration between woodland owners are available.

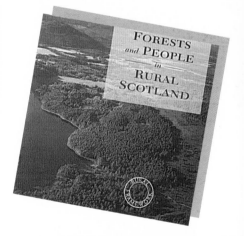

Community Participation in Forest Management

We are keen to enhance the contribution which forestry can make to sustaining rural communities and to consider how to increase the scope for local community participation in forest management, in the light of research commissioned by the Forestry Commission and taking account of the points raised in the FAPIRA discussion document.

Community Woodlands

Through the Community Woodland Supplement to the Woodland Grant Scheme, the Government encourages new woodlands which communities can use for recreation. The Forestry Commission and local authorities have prepared strategic plans for creating new community woodland. Over 1,250 hectares of community woodland have been planted in Scotland close towns and villages since the scheme began in April 1992.

A Sustainable and Economic Future for Fishing

Our policies are based on the recognition that fishing in many parts of Scotland represents a traditional way of life, where the industry works in harmony with the environment. If this lifestyle is to survive into the next century, we must balance the catching of fish, which contributes to the economic viability of coastal towns, with the natural ability of fish stocks to regenerate.

182 The Forestry Commission, in association with The Scottish Office, Highlands and Islands Enterprise and Scottish Natural Heritage, has commissioned Aberdeen University to carry out research into the demand and opportunities for community involvement in forestry. The Scottish Rural Development Forestry Programme, an initiative by a consortium of non-Government organisations, is also active in this field and will lead to appraisals and plans for action by rural communities themselves.

The Future of Forestry

183 Following the Review of Forestry, we published in 1994 the Command Paper *"Our Forests, the Way Ahead"*. This outlined the Government' s plans to help forestry develop to meet the challenges of the 21st century. Forest Enterprise is being set up as an Agency to manage the Forestry Commission's estate. Through its Corporate Plan and Framework Document, specific targets will be set for all its activities and priority is given to recreational, environmental and conservation as well as commercial objectives. We believe that the quality of new woodland is at least as important as the physical area of expansion; and expect forestry expansion in Scotland to provide environmental benefits, through for example, the creation of new native woodlands, as well as increasing timber production in the long term.

FISHERIES

A Key Industry

184 Fishing in rural areas of Scotland can mean anything from hand gatherers collecting cockles from the beaches, through creelers harvesting lobsters in inshore waters, to large trawlers fishing in international waters for cod. Fishing can be a lucrative business - prices range from nearly £10,000 a tonne for lobsters, to over £1,000 a tonne for well-known whitefish species like haddock and plaice. Within 6 miles from the Scottish shoreline only UK vessels are allowed to fish; and there are also strict controls on access to the 6-12 mile zone by fishermen from other European Union countries. These restrictions protect the local interests of Scottish fishermen.

185 Fishing is a key industry in the rural economies of the North-East and the Highlands & Islands. Scotland' s fishing industry handled 71% of all UK fish landings in the UK in 1994, with a market value of some £280 million. Scotland's major fishmarket, Peterhead, is the largest in Europe. Exports are booming - the value of Scottish fish landed directly into other EU countries has risen from £6 million in 1989 to nearly £30 million in 1994; but this is only a small part of the total market for fish products, where the value of UK exports approaches £450 million.

186 The industry is also a vital source of employment in Scotland. There are over 8,500 people directly employed as fishermen, with a further 13,000 employed onshore in fishing-related activities.

Sustainable fishing

187 However, there is an acute European-wide problem of over-capacity as too many boats are catching limited stocks of fish too fast. The industry expanded during the 1980s on the basis of buoyant fish stocks and

Creel fishing

increasing technical efficiency. Fish stocks are now being exploited at or above their level of capacity. To achieve sustainable fishing, the United Kingdom and other European Community Member States are taking joint action within the Common Fisheries Policy to ensure that a secure and profitable fishing industry thrives into the next century.

188 The Government have sought to protect the long-term interests of the Scottish industry by helping fishermen to take their boats out of production through the fishing vessel decommissioning scheme. By March 1995, Scotland had decommissioned 95 vessels and total grants paid out to Scottish fishermen amounted to nearly £5.5 million. A further £12 million was made available to decommission UK boats in the period to March 1996.

189 The Government recognise that the reduction in fishing opportunities has a direct impact on coastal communities. As in other sectors, retraining and income support measures are available to help those who need to seek other employment. In addition to these measures, Scotland will receive some £14 million in EC grant aid under the 1994-99 PESCA Programme, which is designed to encourage fishermen to develop other activities and create job opportunities in local areas.

Fish Farming

190 Salmon farming is one of the most significant new industries to emerge in the Highlands and Islands of Scotland over the past 25 years. It is now an international food commodity which is widely available to the public. In 1994 the aquaculture industry was worth around £220 million to the Scottish economy and provides direct and indirect employment to some 6,000 people. Salmon and shellfish farming is mainly concentrated in the sea-lochs of the west coast, the Western Isles and the sheltered voes and inlets of the Shetland and Orkney Islands. Further expansion in salmon farming in Scotland will depend on it remaining competitive with other producing countries and maintaining the disease-free status of stocks. The

Our Strategy for Salmon

Scotland's wild salmon fisheries are renowned internationally and make an important contribution to Scotland's economy and to the natural heritage. A great deal of knowledge and advice on our salmon and sea trout fisheries is available. In recognition of the importance of these fisheries we have set up an eminent task force to develop, over the next year, a comprehensive strategy for the management of our salmon stocks which will take us into the next century.

We will also publish in the spring of 1996 general guidance on fish farming and the environment in order to ensure that the impact of present and future development on the natural heritage is appropriately managed.

Fish farm, Loch Creran

shortage of suitable near-shore sites could constrain further development but the development of the technology may enable expansion at more exposed offshore locations.

191 Trout farming is confined principally to inland waters of central and lowland Scotland. Although much smaller in scale, it also makes a significant contribution to the rural economy. The farmed shellfish industry is on a relatively small scale but produces high quality, high value products. Trout production for the table as well as for recreational use has potential to expand further in Scotland. The farmed shellfish industry is on a relaitvely small scale but produces high quality, high value products and aslo has considerable potential to meet European demand, and to increase domestic consumption. There is also potential for diversification into other forms of finfish, such as halibut, production. Technological problems are being tackled which may enable other species of finfish to emerge as viable farmed alternatives to salmon and trout over the next 5 to 10 years.

TOURISM

192 Tourism is one of Scotland's most important industries. In 1994, visitor expenditure totalled around £2,000 million of which about £1,450 million was spent outwith the main urban areas of Edinburgh and Glasgow. In many rural areas, tourism is already the largest source of employment; in the Highlands and Islands, for example, tourism provides employment for about 20% of the total workforce and in some areas such as Argyll and Skye it is of considerably greater significance.

193 Tourism offers real prospects of expansion in rural areas. The main attractions of Scotland for tourists are associated with the natural environment, but visitors do require a healthy rural economy. Visitors often want to meet local people and experience local culture. Visitors also need good service in terms of a variety of shops, good transport facilities and good visitor attractions.

Scottish
TOURIST BOARD

Iona ferry

194 In November 1994, the Scottish Tourism Co-ordinating Group published a strategy for Scottish tourism. The Group is chaired by the Minister with responsibility for tourism at The Scottish Office and brings together the main public bodies involved in supporting the tourist industry together with a representative of the industry itself. The key objectives of the strategy are to increase visitor expenditure, develop all year round tourism and develop tourism outwith main tourism areas. The realisation of these objectives would greatly benefit rural areas. For example, more visitors to hotels and restaurants and caravan parks will mean greater local expenditure and improved viability for other industries and services.

195 Protection of the environment is an essential task if tourists are to continue to be attracted to rural areas. The Co-ordinating Group has established a Task Force which brings together private and public sector agencies (including Scottish Natural Heritage) to promote the concept of sustainable tourism. The Task Force has set up throughout Scotland a series of Tourism Management Programmes to demonstrate the advantages of long term management of tourism resources. The lessons of these programmes are to be disseminated widely so that groups elsewhere in Scotland can similarly develop sustainable tourism projects.

TRAVEL IN RURAL AREAS

196 Living and working in rural areas poses obvious challenges, created by distances from the main centres of the population and, within rural areas, between settlements. Distance raises the costs of travel and the time spent travelling. Lower density of population will also affect possibilities for the provision of public transport services, potentially restricting the scope and choice of services available. Our aim must be, wherever possible, to reduce and minimise the difficulties these circumstances pose. Improving access and lowering its cost also aids local economic development and contributes to the policy goal of preventing depopulation in certain rural areas.

Tourism

The key challenges which face Scottish tourism apply to the whole country. It is a diffuse industry, spreading across a number of economic activities and built on many businesses, of which a good number are small.

We reviewed support to tourism in 1993 and as a result published a National Strategic Plan for Scottish Tourism in November 1994 following widespread consultation with the industry. It sets out a framework for action that can be adopted by local interests and adapted to their needs. Its importance is in the focus it gives to the key issues. It proposes as its main objectives to:

● create new and improve existing facilities

● promote tourism in a more effective and co-ordinated way at all levels

● enhance skills

The *Tourism and the Environment Task Force* has been established reflecting the opportunities to develop and promote more imaginative holiday packages based on the natural environment. A growing interest in the environment, natural history and remote places has produced a demand for "green holidays" which Scotland is well placed to serve.

Our Rural Transport Objective

To enhance the accessibility of rural areas, recognising the particular circumstances facing rural travellers and the needs of the rural economy.

197 In partnership with the private sector, central and local government can contribute to improvements in a number of ways. These range from the provision of improved trunk and local roads, support for socially necessary bus services, support for innovative forms of transport, provision and subsidy to Island ferry services and support to airports and lifeline air services. Developments in telecommunications can also reduce the need for travel and can have the effect of shrinking distance.

198 In rural areas, accessibility must, for many, imply use of the car. Car ownership is crucial to mobility in rural areas as the facts show. In 1991, 7 out of every 10 rural households had access to a car, compared with less than half of urban households. The proportion of households with more than one car is also much higher in many rural areas. This reflects the greater need for a car in the absence of alternatives. There are, though, significant groups of people - particularly the young, women and others with low incomes - who do not own cars and can face particular difficulties in rural areas. Action to maintain and, where possible, improve public transport will continue to be necessary.

Transport and the Rural Economy

199 The quality of rural transport services will also affect the rural economy. Better links to wider markets improve export opportunities and widen the diversity of the local economy. Consumers benefit from a wider choice of cheaper goods, in the shops. In particular, good transport access for tourists enhances the ability of Scotland's tourist attractions to be enjoyed by a wide range of domestic and foreign tourists who contribute enormously in terms of local incomes and jobs. Tourists have particular travel needs and the provision of services must adapt to these to enhance business prospects. As 80% of visitors travel by road, good route signing is particularly important. In co-operation with the Scottish Tourist Board, Area Tourist Boards, local authorities and attraction operators the Government have facilitated the introduction of 10 National Tourist Routes to encourage tourists to visit areas off the main through routes, which might otherwise be passed. Research shows these routes are successful and they will be more widely promoted. Recently the Government have taken an initiative to bring together the Scottish Tourist Board, Highlands and Islands Enterprise, Caledonian MacBrayne and Scotrail to discuss ways of improving linkages between transport and tourism in the Highlands. This forum will be expanded to include Highlands and Islands Airports Ltd and the Highlands Area Tourist Board.

Roads

200 Roads are crucial to access in rural areas, and rural economies are critically dependent on road transport for conveying production materials and finished goods. The Scottish Office has sustained a very high commitment to the development of the National Road Network. It is now possible to make return trips in a day which would have been unthinkable 20 or 30 years ago. Consequently rural areas benefit significantly from enhanced accessibility and quicker communication. The A9, the A90, A74(M), the A1 and the A96 all serve large areas of rural Scotland. The major upgradings of these routes over the last 20 years have been outstanding achievements, as have the improvements to the A75 (the strategic link between the

Skye Bridge

A fixed link to Skye provides effective and reliable transport system that is vitally important to islands such as Skye which face particular problems of remoteness and sparse distribution of population. The New Roads and Streetworks Act 1991 provided the framework for the provision of a privately funded bride to Skye to greatly enhance the ferry service much sooner than could have been achieved from the publicly funded roads programme.

The Skye Bridge contract was the first scheme in the UK to be promoted and constructed under provisions of the 1991 Act. Construction, valued at over £24 million, started in July 1992 and the bridge opened in mid-October. With the inclusion of the A956 Kyleakin to Uig road into the trunk road network from April 1996, the bridge will form part of a more direct link to the Western Isles.

mainland motorway network and the Northern Ireland ferry port at Stranraer) and the A830 Mallaig road.

201 These improvements not only facilitate access but also make a tangible contribution to eliminating feelings of isolation and remoteness in very large areas of rural Scotland. The substantial capital resources made available to local authorities in the past decade to develop the local road infrastructure have also contributed to significantly enhanced communication. The resultant savings in transportation costs to rural businesses are substantial and have been of great importance in the development of industry and the economy of rural Scotland.

Village Gates, Langholm

Road Safety

202 The high quality of scenery and environment in Scotland's rural areas attracts many tourists. This has implications for road safety as visitors may be unfamiliar with the routes or in a hurry to reach the next attraction. Measures have been introduced to treat a significant number of sites where serious road accidents have taken place in the past. On the A9 Perth to Inverness route, where several accidents have involved foreign drivers, a publicity leaflet has been made available in several languages giving advice about good driving practice. Together with police speed limit enforcement, initiatives such as the "Speedwatch" campaigns and the installation of speed cameras also contribute towards the achievement of the Government's target of reducing road accident casualties by a third compared with the 1981-85 average by the year 2000.

203 There is scope for some growth in road traffic in rural areas without severe environmental, health or congestion problems. Nevertheless, some rural communities already suffer from adverse traffic impacts. These are being addressed through improved road design, sign-posting and the routing of lorry traffic to avoid sensitive areas.

204 Traffic calming of trunk roads through rural towns and villages helps preserve their quality of life and their attractiveness to visitors and is one of the issues addressed in The Scottish Office Route Action Plans. The purpose of such measures is to slow down through traffic thus providing a safer environment for those who live in rural areas. Many of these towns and villages have a remarkable degree of local character and regional identity. It is important that traffic calming schemes are designed with special care as it is easy to mar unintentionally the quality of this distinction.

Public Transport

205 Buses are, and are likely to remain, the most widely used form of public transport in the countryside. Almost all bus services are provided by private operators. The role of local authorities is to subsidise routes where they consider this to be socially desirable. Information about time-tabling of routes and the connections between different forms of transport such as buses, trains and ferries is crucial in rural Scotland. The provision of better travel information is an area where new technology can and does make a real difference. Highland Regional Council, supported by Highlands and Islands Enterprise and the Scottish Tourist Board are planning to develop

Village Gates: Langholm

The new "gateways" at the entrances to the Borders town of Langholm on the A7 trunk road, part of a package of traffic calming measures planned to ease problems in the town, show what can be achieved by partnership between local people, businesses and local government and The Scottish Office. Designed by local children in a competition arranged by The Scottish Office National Roads Directorate, and implemented by artist Fiona McColl, who also secured funding from two major businesses in the town, the gateways depict well-known local images and features. It is hoped that they will encourage other towns and villages where traffic calming schemes are proposed in raising the quality of such schemes.

Railway line, west of Edinburgh

and produce maps and a series of timetable books which together will provide a comprehensive guide to transport in the Highlands & Islands Enterprise area. The provision of better information will help tourists and locals alike in maximising the use of existing services. Assistance has also been provided through the Rural Transport Innovation Grant Scheme which was set up to encourage innovative approaches for the provision of public transport services to benefit those living or working in rural areas.

206 Post buses in Scotland play a key role in providing vital transport links in the most isolated rural areas. Since the service was launched in 1968 the network has grown to over 140 routes. Grant assistance is available from The Scottish Office which has, in particular, aided the acquisition of post bus vehicles in Highland Region, where many services also double as school buses for local children.

207 Rail travel is important in some areas of rural Scotland, and ferries and air services are the lifeblood of the island communities. In addition to regional travel they facilitate direct access to Scotland's major cities and beyond. Many rural transport services will never be commercially viable. That is why subsidy will continue to be available for socially necessary services. In addition - under the franchising arrangements - users of rural rail services will for the first time have the benefit of contractually binding guarantees for levels of service. The guarantees will safeguard services on every line and to every station in the country. Moreover, our commitment to regulating rail fares will mean that key rail fares will increase by no more than inflation for the next 3 years and will decrease in real terms for 4 years thereafter.

208 Privatisation and franchising offer new opportunities to enhance the use of lines and stations. Private sector operators will have incentives to provide innovative services to encourage the use of rural lines and flexibility to

Islay airport

increase service provision where they judge it to be in their interests to do so. There will also be opportunities for partnerships between the private sector and local government to develop new schemes to enhance or to reopen lines and stations.

209 For many island communities ferries represent the main, if not only means, of communication and transport to neighbouring islands and the mainland. We have emphasised the importance we attach to these by our commitment to continue support for ferry services which are necessary to maintain and improve the social and economic development of the islands. Essential roll-on/roll-off ferry services to Orkney and Shetland will soon be safeguarded by a long-term guarantee, for the first time ever. A contract between the operator and The Scottish Office will bind the operator to provide a specified frequency and pattern of services over several years. Tenders are soon to be invited from shipping operators to provide ferry services under the new arrangements and it is expected that the contract will be awarded in spring of 1996. The network of approved services provided by the Government-owned company Caledonian MacBrayne to islands off the west coast of Scotland will also remain supported by long-term Government subsidy.

210 Air services provide an equally vital economic and social link, for many island communities, providing access to urban centres for financial, commercial, and other services not available locally. We will continue to make available financial support for the Glasgow-Tiree-Barra lifeline air service, which cannot be provided commercially. In addition, subsidy will continue to be paid to ensure the continuation of operations at the 9 airports in the Highland and Islands, currently managed by another Government company, Highlands and Islands Airports Ltd, in order to maintain transport links and to enhance the well-being and viability of the communities served.

211 The ownership of Highlands and Islands Airports Ltd was transferred from the Civil Aviation Authority to the Secretary of State on 1 April 1995. The transfer brings all strategic policy decisions regarding operations and

finance within the responsibility of the Secretary of State for Scotland. There will be a continuing need for subsidy from The Scottish Office to cover operating losses and to secure the future of those company's airports which are not commercially viable. The Secretary of State has taken immediate steps to enhance the value obtained for that subsidy and the benefits which the airports bring to the Highlands & Islands by exploring the potential contribution of the private sector, through an independent review.

Radio Fixed Access Provision in Rural Areas

Scottish rural areas will benefit under Government proposals to extend competition in telecommunications services to customers through the use of radio fixed access, also known as the "local loop", the final connection between customers and the local switching centre.

● Radio offers a way to meet the demand for fast information highway links in remote rural areas where the cost of laying fibre-optic cable would be prohibitive;

● Although the Highlands and Islands are already well served (80% of working population) up to ISDN level as a result of the BT and Highlands & Islands Enterprise initiative, the new proposal should mean an improved communications service in the Borders and parts of Dumfries and Galloway;

● The proposal will particularly benefit the increasing number of people who telework from small villages who want better access to more advanced telecommunications services in order to extend the scope of their work.

EUROPEAN INFLUENCES

212 Over the next few years, Scotland's rural areas will be receiving more support from the European Structural Funds than ever before. During the 1993 review of areas eligible to receive Structural Funds across the European Community, we were successful in arguing the case for greatly extending Scottish Objective 5b coverage (to promote rural economic development) to include the whole of the Dumfries & Galloway and Borders Regions and large areas within Grampian, Tayside and Central Regions. In addition the Highlands & Islands were upgraded to Objective 1.

213 Taken with an additional £16.5 million secured through the LEADER II Initiative (focused directly on rural development and, in particular, encouraging innovative approaches at local level), some £390 million of European Community support will be made available for boosting rural economic development in Scotland over the period until 1999. This contribution from the European Community will only part fund projects. It must be, at least, matched by project sponsors in the eligible areas, bringing the total value of the programme to around £800 million. These sponsors will normally include local authorities, local enterprise companies, Scottish Natural Heritage, further education colleges and voluntary sector organisations. The initiative for proposing and developing potential European funded projects lies with the local community and these potential funders.

214 European aid will be targetted at the specific economic development needs of each eligible area but, in general, will focus on supporting small and medium-sized businesses and business infrastructure, tourism, training, communications, environmental action and agricultural diversification.

The Prospects

215 The evidence is strong for a continuing lively economy in rural Scotland. Its pattern will change, still firmly rooted in the land, but becoming an economy more based on the delivery of services than on producing basic materials. It will succeed by continuing to exploit its natural assets, by exploring its diversity and by seizing the opportunities which are so clearly within its grasp.

SHAPING PARTNERSHIPS

OUR AIMS FOR RURAL SCOTLAND

216 The rural communities of Scotland are a vibrant, distinctive and vital part of Scotland. Their population is almost one-third of Scotland and the land in which they live is one of the most significant assets of the United Kingdom, in terms of landscape, natural heritage and the economic activities like tourism and agriculture which they support. They form a thriving modern rural society dispersed over a large area.

217 The Government believe that, first and foremost, the future of rural Scotland rests with, and should rest with, the people and businesses who live there. They are best placed to understand what is most needed in their particular communities.

Upland land use, Loch Tayside

The Role of Individuals and Community Institutions

218 It is one of the characteristics of rural communities that they come together in varying patterns, around a variety of nuclei, and under the influence of a wide range of cohesive forces. Each community is different, and individuals can make a real difference to whether particular rural communities are successful in realising their ambitions or not. The Government believe in encouraging individual initiative and strengthening grass-roots local institutions so that rural communities are able to shape their own future.

Churches In Rural Communities

Church involvement in rural communities is varied and depends on the individual members of the congregation making their contribution, which is constrained by small congregational numbers and remoteness. Money is an important factor but not as important as the individuals and their role. For example, the Episcopal Church seeks to work with all age groups in the community, from babies and toddlers with the creation of mother and toddler groups, pre-school playgroups and after school clubs, to pensioners by providing day care and community transport for the elderly. It offers counselling and befriending schemes and family centres. Some training and employment programmes and youth clubs for young people are provided and it is involved with local councils, community and village hall associations, and housing associations. Such involvement with a housing association led to church land being developed into rented houses prompted by the needs of the community.

West Linton Church

219 In many communities, the church is an important factor, providing assistance and advice beyond that of its immediate pastoral responsibilities. The church hall is often the only communal meeting place for the rural community, whether for sales of work, discussion of a new development or a ceilidh. In crofting communities, the township clerk provides another focus and in others, the local shopkeeper, who may have come from very far away, will often seek to promote the interests of the community. In Aberfeldy, it was the pursuit of sustainable tourism which brought unlikely interests together, but led on to new fields such as broadcasting. The imminent demise of the Laggan village shop set off many ventures. Every successful rural community has, at its heart, some force around which the community adheres and develops. In every case that force draws its power from the community itself.

220 This cohesion is assisted by the hundreds of local and wider circulation newspapers and magazines in Scotland, many with long and distinguished histories. The broadcasting organisations deliver programming which reflects the special characteristics of their areas. Rural Scotland has an image, beyond that of the kilt and heather, which appeals to a world-wide audience. It is an image, based in fact, of real rural communities which continue to prosper drawing on local skills and resources and taking their strength from the independent and strongly expressed views of their people.

The Role of the New Councils

221 Government, both at national and local level, should be responsive to the needs of local communities and work with them to help them achieve their aims. Local authorities have a particularly important part to play since their councillors are elected locally and are well placed to reflect local views and ensure that policies and service delivery are attuned to local circumstances. But, for long, there has been confusion in the minds of many about which council, region or district, dealt with which services. Similarly, members of the public have had difficulty in determining which councillor they should approach if they had a problem. The creation of

The *"Make a Difference"* Initiative

Volunteering has a vital role to play in the life of rural communities where people can be remote from services. Volunteers can bring significant social, economic and personal values to local communities. The range and extent of volunteering in rural communities in Scotland is well known, especially though such organisations as the Scottish Women's Rural Institutes and the Scottish Women's Royal Voluntary Service. As part of its Make a Difference Initiative, the Government wishes to encourage volunteering in all aspects of life.

The report *"Make a Difference: An Outline Volunteering Strategy for the UK"*, published in June 1995, was produced by a team drawn from the volunteering, public and private sectors: it made 81 recommendations for strengthening and enhancing volunteering. Key elements of the Government's response to the report include Youth Challenge which will provide:

- a volunteering opportunity by the end of 1997 to all 15-25 year olds in the United Kingdom who wish to volunteer

- funding for 50 innovative projects throughout the United Kingdom which will help develop volunteering by young and older people

- a national media campaign to promote volunteering

- a new *Make a Difference Award* to acknowledge volunteering.

A Scottish Office Task Force has been established to consider how best the recommendations can be taken forward throughout Scotland. The Task Force will look to increasing the opportunities for young people to volunteer and to extending the network of volunteer bureaux throughout Scotland. This will build on the work presently being carried out by Volunteer Development Scotland through four Scottish Office funded pilot volunteer projects which are testing various methods of encouraging greater numbers of volunteers and matching them with relevant volunteering opportunities. These projects have a rural or island focus:

- a network project throughout Highland Region involving nine councils of voluntary service to examine the problems involved in providing opportunities for volunteering in geographically disadvantaged areas;

- a partnership project based in Dumfries with an outreach centre in Upper Nithsdale providing volunteering opportunities with a council of voluntary service;

- a volunteer information and placement project in the Isle of Lewis

- a project for Stirling and its surrounding rural areas is looking at the development of a "portable" service approach which could be used to make volunteering more accessible to rural areas.

All projects will run until at least March 1997. The lessons learned from the projects will help to develop the *Make a Difference* initiative to strengthen the volunteering network throughout Scotland, particularly in rural areas.

unitary authorities on 1 April 1996, will change that: members of the public will have one council, one councillor. Of importance, particularly in rural areas, councils will be able to approach services in an integrated and comprehensive way: no longer will housing and social work and education and leisure be the responsibility of separate councils.

222 The new councils will combine the functions of district and regional councils. The existing 53 district and 9 regional councils on the mainland will be replaced by 29 unitary authorities but the 3 island councils for Western Isles, Orkney and Shetland will largely remain unchanged. Three new public authorities will be created for water and sewerage services, which will be monitored by new a Scottish Water and Sewerage Customers Council. There will be a new Scottish Children's Reporter Administration.

223 The restructuring of local government is not simply about single tier authorities. Section 23 of the Local Government etc (Scotland) Act 1994 requires that all new councils must prepare by 1 April 1997 schemes for decentralisation. This will bring councils nearer to the communities they serve (both physically and philosophically) and involve the communities more closely in the policy and decision-making processes undertaken on their behalf.

Care Assistant in Grantown on Spey

224 Decentralisation offers rural communities, in particular, the opportunity to overcome what has been described as the "remoteness" of local councils. In drawing up their schemes of decentralisation, councils will be required to consult community councils in their area and other interested parties. The Government believe that these bodies have a significant and worthwhile contribution to make to the running of local affairs: one which, founded on close proximity, can provide a more focused and accurate reflection of local needs and aspirations and engender even greater community self confidence and unity.

225 The Government believe that there is too much involvement of central Government in the detailed implementation of local authority business and will look for areas where central reporting requirements or centrally imposed burdens can be eased. The aim will be to have more devolution of power to local government. In turn, the new councils should consider, before embarking on any new venture, whether this can be done better by some other organisation and whether there are potential partners who would assist towards its success.

226 In rural areas, there are special problems that have to be overcome in the delivery of services, in particular remoteness and sparsity of population. We have asked the new councils to prepare decentralisation strategies designed to enable local people to have greater control over the way in which their needs are met. This move towards decentralisation can also be seen in changes to the way that the major agencies are organised. Scottish Homes, the Enterprise network, Scottish Natural Heritage and The Scottish Office, through its new system of local agricultural officers, have all set up arrangements for local decision-making, within strategies set by each body. The time is now right to move that process a stage further, by finding ways to encourage linkages between these bodies working at

local level, in order to achieve the best in terms of value for money, avoiding duplication and, most importantly, joining forces with the local community.

227 This kind of linkage is already being put in place in rural Scotland. The *Tayside Rural Strategy Group* is an example of local bodies, led by the Regional Council in this case, getting together to agree a strategy for the area. On a smaller scale, the *Rural Stirling Partnership* uses an approach that seeks to maximise the contribution that each individual body can make to the area. We believe that the success of these initiatives must now be built upon and encouraged more widely.

The Role of Government

228 From many points of view, the policies which Government offers to rural communities need be no different in their fundamentals to those which apply to towns and cities although, as we have demonstrated, the application of these policies needs to be tailored to the circumstances, whether hill or glen, island or forest.

229 There have been substantial achievements in the last three years in enabling those responsible for serving the rural community to understand its needs. Many organisations are now taking up the partnership approach, recognising that it is not an empty concept but a practical tool for working towards shared objectives. We have done this ourselves, through the establishment of the Rural Focus Group whose progress report is published with this document. The rural population has made its views known, both in the preparation for this White Paper and in many other contexts. One clear common view is that it is vital that change, where it is needed, comes from the community itself, and is not imposed from outside. It is the function of central Government to provide the framework within which the greatest freedoms can exist to pursue opportunity while, at the same time, offering care and protection for those unable to go ahead alone.

230 We believe that, in order to provide a broad framework within which a partnership approach can be taken forward, it would now be useful to set down the overall aims of our policies for rural Scotland. Such a statement of the overall aims of rural policy has never been made before. We believe these aims, which reflect the consultations we have carried out for this White Paper, will be widely shared by the people of rural Scotland. They will also assist various parts of Government, the national agencies, local authorities and others to co-ordinate their efforts in the interests of rural communities. Our overall aims for rural Scotland are set out in this document.

231 The four arms of this policy framework - economic, social, cultural, environmental - are each vital to our vision for the future of rural Scotland. We have looked at aspects of our current policies in each quadrant in previous chapters. There are, of course, differences in the circumstances of particular rural areas as a result of geography and history, and resource and other constraints will affect the speed with which progress can be made. But, in principle, the Government believe that all four dimensions need to be achieved, and that they are mutually reinforcing. The overall

The Hermitage, River Braan

The Government's Policies for the Rural Communities of Scotland

We will work in partnership to enable rural Scotland to be:

● economically prosperous, with a range of job opportunities which will enable those who live in rural communities, native or newcomer, to enjoy worthwhile ways of life.

● vigorous in its community life supported by good local infrastructure and quality services.

● culturally confident, cherishing local traditions and distinctive ways of life, and able to adapt to and benefit from changing circumstances.

● able to protect, conserve and enhance its outstanding natural environment.

aim of the our rural policy is to work, in partnership with others, towards the achievement of this vision.

THE SCOTTISH RURAL PARTNERSHIP

232 We are determined now to give power to the concept of partnership in rural areas. The basic elements are in place, with the growing consensus in rural communities on what needs to be done, the establishment of devolved working by many national agencies, decentralisation by the new councils and the national Rural Focus Group. We propose to bring these together in a new *Scottish Rural Partnership*. This will have three main components:

- *Scottish Local Rural Partnerships;*

- *The Scottish National Rural Partnership;*

- *The Scottish Rural Partnership Fund.*

Scottish Local Rural Partnerships

233 While machinery is in place at national level to foster an integrated approach to rural policy, for example the Rural Focus Group, there is considerable scope for strengthening partnership working at a more local level. This is a theme which emerged strongly from the consultations carried out for this White Paper. There are already many examples of local partnerships for particular purposes, as described in the progress report by the Rural Focus Group, but we believe the time is now right to encourage local partnerships on a wider front.

234 Local partnerships, both in terms of the bodies represented on them, and the issues they address, should reflect local circumstances. It would be wrong to attempt to impose a single model on the vast range of different circumstances throughout rural Scotland. But the key commitments should be:

- **putting the needs and priorities of rural communities first;**

- **Government, agencies, local authorities, and the voluntary and private sectors, working together in an integrated way.**

235 The Government will encourage and assist local rural partnerships through:-

- **publishing guidance on how local partnerships might operate;**

- **establishing a new *Scottish Rural Partnership Fund* to provide pump-priming assistance to local partnerships;**

- **promoting a programme of research on the identification and dissemination of good practice in local rural development.**

236 We will shortly publish more detailed guidance on these issues. We expect that the *Local Rural Partnerships* would work on a range of issues for the area

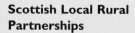

Scottish Local Rural Partnerships

We will encourage and assist the establishment of Local Rural Partnerships drawn from the most relevant local interests, providing a basis for making local input to decisions affecting local areas.

Spittal Quarry, near Wick

concerned, depending on local priorities. Topics that existing local partnerships have considered include:

● **improving the prospects for economic development in the area;**

● **issues relating to land use planning;**

● **the delivery of local services in a way most geared to local needs;**

● **local transport;**

● **ways to encourage the most sustainable use of the natural resources of the area.**

237 The membership of the local partnership should reflect the kinds of issues that it wishes to cover and the body that leads the partnership will similarly be the most appropriate to local circumstances. We expect that the new councils would certainly be represented on the local partnership and that representatives of the local communities would also be included, through community councils or other relevant groups.

238 The basic functions of local partnerships might include:

● **preparing a local strategy, taking stock of the overall needs and priorities for rural development in the local area and the policies available to achieve this; perhaps drawing on the work local authorities are doing on Local Agenda 21 plans;**

● **considering the scope for more effective local service delivery, including opportunities for joint working between the partners, shared use of buildings or other resources and a more integrated approach to providing information to local people about the services and assistance available;**

● **providing a focus for promoting and responding to community-led initiatives.**

239 *Local Rural Partnerships* would operate on a voluntary basis and each prospective partner would need to decide what staff resources could be committed to further the aims of the partnership. The partnerships would have to operate within the framework of established national policies, for example, on agriculture and forestry.

240 As well as including representatives of local communities, they would work with the community groups of various kinds which already exist in most parts of rural Scotland, including, for example, Scottish Women's Rural Institutes, local farmers' groups, community associations and various bodies formed to cover particular interests. The aim would be to reflect the needs and wishes of local residents and to encourage local people to undertake their own projects and initiatives for their area.

Tore Mill, Inverness

Rural Action Network

● Rural Forum has recently begun the development of a networking service to support those people working with the disadvantaged in Rural Scotland. *Rural Action Network* will be piloted in two areas of rural Scotland, with an initial membership of 150 and a central administration and coordination base, located in Perth.

● The service will consist of an information resource, available through computer networks; support and technical assistance, through for example specialised training and the establishment of a Local Exchange Trading System to encourage resource sharing; and demonstration and action research projects.

● It will provide a mechanism for support and communication for community agents already in the field and help identify gaps in this type of service. Membership of the Network will be open across Scotland and services outside the two pilot areas will be made available incrementally.

The Arkleton Centre for Rural Development Research

The new Arkleton Centre for Rural Development Research in Aberdeen aims to become a centre of excellence for rural development research and teaching on a decentralised basis throughout rural Scotland.

241 Each *Local Rural Partnership* would find its own way of achieving this kind of local involvement. Experience from the LEADER programme and elsewhere suggests that successful community-based development is labour intensive. In many cases the use of animateurs or community development agents can be helpful in giving communities the leadership and confidence to pursue their own objectives. There is already a large number of such community development agents at work in rural Scotland. They are often local people who know the area and its residents well and, frequently on a voluntary basis, have taken the lead in representing local views when the occasion arises. The *Local Rural Partnerships* might encourage greater community involvement by:

- **offering wider opportunities for communities to have a voice in decision-making, through representation on committees, community-led exercises, participation projects;**

- **ensuring that sufficient information and expertise is available to local people on sources of funding, opportunities for involvement and making their views known, including the employment of officers dedicated to that task;**

- **taking stock of existing community development agents and considering the need for increased numbers of these, perhaps employed by one of the partners, or through support for existing services;**

- **setting out the remit of community development agents, in terms of encouraging the formation of community groups, taking forward community projects on behalf of the partners and representing the needs and wishes of communities;**

- **identifying training for existing animateurs, through community education and other services.**

242 Many agencies outside Government have been working hard to achieve greater self-awareness for rural communities. A number of partnership arrangements are described in *"Rural Focus: Progress Since Framework"* published simultaneously with this document.

The Scottish National Rural Partnership

The Scottish National Rural Partnership

We will establish a national body, building on the success of the Rural Focus Group, and providing coordination of national action to match that undertaken by the *Local Rural Partnerships*.

243 Building on the firm foundation provided by the *Rural Focus Group,* we now propose to establish the *Scottish National Rural Partnership* whose work should include:

- **as its main task, support and advice to the local *Rural Partnership Groups;***

- **encouraging and co-ordinating the establishment of local rural partnerships throughout Scotland;**

- **advising Ministers on the disbursement of the new *Scottish Rural Partnership Fund;***

- keeping under review progress towards the overall aims of rural policy;

- sponsoring and overseeing a programme of research, using the wealth of relevant talent in Scotland, with the aim of identifying and disseminating information on good practice in local rural development.

244 Its membership would be based on that of the Rural Focus Group, but we will consider whether membership should be extended in some areas, for example a strengthened representation of the main land-owning and land-user groups. We would look for continued commitment from each of its constituent bodies reinforced by an annual meeting of the chairs of each organisation to review achievements over the past year and to determine the programme for the next.

245 We recognise that it is for Government to take a lead in the development of the Scottish Rural Partnership network. Following publication of more detailed guidance, we will work with other rural organisations to mount a major conference in the spring of 1996 to bring together rural communities, Government agencies, the private sector and voluntary groups to pool expertise and concert action.

The Scottish Rural Partnership Fund

246 In order to assist the formation of local rural partnerships, and to encourage local community involvement, we will set up a *Scottish Rural Partnership Fund* to:

- bring together a number of existing small grant schemes relevant to rural Scotland;

- offer financial support to projects proposed by local rural partnerships on behalf of communities;

- part fund the initial costs incurred in developing local rural partnerships.

247 The Scottish Office offers a number of small grant schemes relevant to rural Scotland. We propose to bring the administration of these schemes together to enable a more strategic approach to be taken. In addition to continuing the funding programmes of the existing schemes the new fund would offer:

- a *Rural Challenge Fund* which will support projects proposed by local rural partnerships on behalf of local community groups, with the emphasis on innovative projects or those that because of their small size or nature might not interest or fall between other funding agencies;

- assistance to local partnerships for secretarial and administrative costs;

- a contribution towards the employment of community development agents by local rural partners;

The Scottish Rural Partnership Fund

Providing resources to support the new groups, contributing to the costs of servicing them, assisting the employment of community development agents, contributing to the funding of consultancies and filling gaps not covered by the wide range of existing support.

The Existing Grant Schemes

The Special Grants (Environmental) Programme is designed to assist Scottish voluntary environmental organisations to improve their overall capability and effectiveness in carrying out environmental, conservation or improvement work.

The Rural Transport Innovation Grant aims to encourage innovative approaches to the provision of local public transport services for the benefit of people living or working in rural areas.

Funding for rural and semi-rural Councils of Voluntary Service which support social welfare voluntary organisations.

Interactive shopping on the Internet

- support for the training of community development agents, through community education services, resources such as the Arkleton Centre or locally-decided means.

248 The resources which can be made available for the new Rural Partnership Fund will be determined in the annual Public Expenditure Survey.

IMPROVING INFORMATION FOR RURAL SCOTLAND

249 We are committed to improving the flow of information to people in rural Scotland about the assistance and services available to them. With electronic communications, distance no longer needs to be the disadvantage for rural Scotland that was once the case. Improved information on, for example, the existing standards of public services, and on financial incentives available for various kinds of activity, is a prerequisite for informed choice and community-based rural development. The Government have already taken a number of initiatives, and we look to build on these through the *Scottish Rural Partnership* in future.

250 We intend that publicly-funded services, whether the responsibility of central or local government, should be fully available to rural dwellers, including the least well-off and others without their own transport. Where the population is dispersed, service providers will not always be as close to all their customers as they are in cities. Rural people know and understand this. No less than those in towns, however, they are entitled to reasonable provision and to high quality services provided efficiently.

251 The Citizen's Charter programme aims to improve standards of public service. The publication of national charters such as the Parents' and Patients' Charters is already transforming the way in which service providers approach their task. We now propose to promote a Rural Charter Checklist with the aim of ensuring that the needs of the people of rural Scotland are fully taken into account in the delivery of public services.

252 We are also keen to promote improved information in rural areas about the range of financial and other assistance available in rural Scotland. The Rural Focus Group has overseen a project which aims to produce an information booklet, similar to that produced by Tayside Regional Council, for other parts of rural Scotland. Rural Forum was commissioned to prepare a national template for this initiative and is working with local authorities with a view to the preparation of local editions for publication when the new councils take control in April 1996. If the new councils proceed with publication it is hope that the booklets would be available during 1996.

253 There has been growing recognition in the public sector of the potential of information highways to increase business competitiveness. The term "information highways" is usually taken to mean the transfer of large amounts of information, including video, still images, audio and text, at high speed between users. The impact of this technology in rural areas could be dramatic, overcoming geographical remoteness from business markets and, through teleworking, enabling people to work while remaining in their home communities.

254 The significance of information highways to the Scottish economy has been seized by Scottish Enterprise which, in collaboration with local enterprise

companies and Highlands and Islands Enterprise, has set up the SPAN (Smart Partnerships Across Networks) initiative to foster business applications of the technology.

255 We recognise the need to provide for the cohesive force which is fundamental to successful rural initiatives. As a small contribution to this and to assist rural communities to take advantage of the potential of the superhighway, this document is being published simultaneously in The Scottish Office pages of the World Wide Web. Many of the other documents referred to here in the *Rural Framework* series will be made available there. We shall be supporting communications within the *Scottish Rural Partnership* through the Internet and a contact address is given at the end of this document. We expect that bulletin boards and many other useful data will be made available to rural communities in this way.

CONCLUSION

256 Taken together, we believe that the three elements of the new *Scottish Rural Partnership* will go a long way towards meeting the needs of rural communities in Scotland for empowerment and local action. These proposals are not intended to and do not cut across the responsibilities of the new councils nor of the existing Government agencies. They are intended to assist those existing bodies to handle the issues arising in rural areas at a scale proportionate to the communities which they serve.

257 They would ensure that decision-making is delegated to the most appropriate level and secure a key role for local authorities, as the democratically elected local bodies, in taking forward development for their area. Now, a framework will be provided which, through best practice, training and modest financial incentives, will enable and facilitate local initiatives and partnerships to be formed on a flexible basis, appropriate to local circumstances. Additional support through other initiatives will also be available and we will seek ways to encourage links between the *Scottish Rural Partnership* and the work of others.

258 In 1992 we set out in *Rural Framework* ideas based on enabling the people of Scotland's rural communities to talk to each other. The future of rural communities in Scotland must be determined by the people of those communities and those who join them to pursue a livelihood, or simply to enjoy their peace and tranquillity. We have pursued developments in Scotland which have been tailored carefully to their needs, assisting and enabling rather than imposing systems devised for other areas.

259 We will continue to work to the objectives set out in this White Paper, in partnership, seeking prosperity for the people of the rural communities of Scotland.

Edinburgh 1995

SPAN

will offer a partnership approach on the superhighway, in particular:

● the development of demonstration projects to present some of the possible applications to businesses;

● a series of awareness-raising seminars to run from autumn 1995 to spring 1996;

● an independent expert advice service and source of information for businesses interested in applying the technology to enhance their own operations.

Scottish Rural Partnership on the Internet

The Scottish Office will be exploring the benefits which the superhighway can bring to rural communities through increasing use of the Internet and World Wide Web.

Further Information

260 If you would like further information or wish to offer views on any matter in this document, initially you should contact:

Ms Linda Sinclair
Rural Affairs & Natural Heritage
The Scottish Office Agriculture, Environment and Fisheries Department
Pentland House
47 Robb's Loan
EDINBURGH
EH14 1TY

Telephone: 0131 244 3159
Fax: 0131 244 4071
E-Mail: ranh.so.ph@gtnet.gov.uk

Contacting Us by E-Mail

261 Communications on the following subject areas can be sent to the Email addresses below:

Scottish National Rural Partnerships: **srpnat.so.ph@gtnet.gov.uk**
Scottish Local Rural Partnerships: **srploc.so.ph@gtnet.gov.uk**
Scottish Rural Partnership Fund: **srpfund.so.ph@gtnet.gov.uk**
Other White Paper Issues: **srwp.so.ph@gtnet.gov.uk**

Information on the Internet

262 We are placing the main documents on the Internet.
This White Paper "Rural Scotland" can be found at:
http://www.hmsoinfo.gov.uk/hmso/document/r-scot/r-scot.htm

"Rural Framework: A Progress Report" is at:
http://www.hmsoinfo.gov.uk/hmso/document/r-frame/r-frame.htm

and "The White Paper Consultation: the Rural Forum Report" can be found at:
http://www.hmsoinfo.gov.uk/hmso/document/r-forum/r-forum.htm

THE FIRST YEAR'S ACTION PROGRAMME

We summarise here the steps we plan to take in the first year following publication of the White Paper.

The Government's Policies for the Rural Communities of Scotland

We will work in partnership and within the objectives of sustainable development to enable rural Scotland to be:

- **economically prosperous, with a range of job opportunities which will enable those who live in rural communities, native or newcomer, to enjoy worthwhile ways of life.**

- **vigorous in its community life supported by good local infrastructure and quality services.**

- **culturally confident, cherishing local traditions and distinctive ways of life, and able to adapt to and benefit from changing circumstances.**

- **able to protect, conserve and enhance its outstanding natural environment.**

THE SCOTTISH RURAL PARTNERSHIP

Scottish Local Rural Partnerships

We will encourage and assist the establishment of *Local Rural Partnerships* drawn from the most relevant local interests, providing a basis for making local input to decisions affecting local areas.

The Scottish National Rural Partnership

We will establish a national body, building on the success of the Rural Focus Group, and providing coordination of national action to match that undertaken by the *Local Rural Partnerships*.

The Scottish Rural Partnership Fund

We will establish the fund which will use a challenge funding approach to provide resources to support the new groups, contributing to the costs of servicing them, assisting the employment of community development agents, contributing to the funding of consultancies and filling gaps not covered by the wide range of existing support.

Guidance on the Scottish Rural Partnership

We will publish guidance on the operation of local partnerships and the new Rural Partnership Fund. This will be part of the overall support we intend to give to the establishment of the *Scottish Rural Partnership* system.

Scottish Rural Partnership on the Internet

We will be exploring the benefits which the superhighway can bring to rural communities through increasing use of the Internet and World Wide Web.

The Rural Charter Checklist

Within the framework of the Citizen's Charter, we will ask the Scottish National Rural Partnership to consult on and prepare a Rural Services Charter Checklist for Scotland which will assist service providers to assess whether they are meeting the needs of rural people and make changes to improve rural services.

PROGRESS SINCE FRAMEWORK

Rural Framework: A Progress Report

The work of the Rural Focus Group is described in *"Rural Framework: A Progress Report"* which is published simultaneously with the White Paper.

Reporting the Consultations

Rural Forum organised the consultation exercise across Scotland. Its report on the consultation and the many helpful and interesting things said in that process is published as *"The White Paper Consultation: the Rural Forum Report"*.

RURAL LIFE

Scottish Rural Life 1995

A new edition of *Scottish Rural Life* will be published incorporating information drawn from the 1991 Census.

"Living in Rural Scotland"

We will publish the report commissioned on rural services.

Access to Information and Advice

We will publish the results of research on how access to information and advice might be improved. Tayside Regional Council's booklet on rural grants, which was sponsored by the Scottish Agricultural College, will be extended to cover the whole of rural Scotland, with assistance from The Scottish Office.

Change in Small Schools

We will fund new research on "The Management of Change, including Devolved School Management, in Small Primary Schools".

Rural Crime

We will mount a study of crime in rural areas and its effect on local people.

PROSPECTS FOR PROSPERITY

Keeping the Shop Open

We intend to bring forward a scheme to reduce the burden of rates on the village shop which is providing a service to isolated communities.

A Rural Business Use Class

In order to ensure that the planning system continues to play its full part in business development we intend to include proposals for a Rural Business Use Class in the consultation on the Use Classes Order.

Rural Business Units

We are considering the case that commercial activities associated with a rural estate whose predominant activity is husbandry should be assessed as a single trading unit for income tax, capital gains tax and inheritance tax purposes.

Opening Up Rural Opportunities

We will produce guidance on rural development intended to encourage positive provision for employment and community purposes using the development plan and control systems. We will also issue guidance on planning for small towns in rural areas covering.

Planning Careers

We are planning a conference on the issues and problems facing rural careers offices in Scotland. It will involve careers service staff from rural areas, local enterprise companies and others and offer the opportunity to share good practice, to identify and address problem areas and explore possible solutions.

Rural Water and Sewerage Grants

In place of the previous grant schemes, we have placed on the new Water Authorities a specific duty to have regard especially to the interests of rural customer and we will take account of this duty in providing resources to the Authorities. Thus the interests of rural customers will be central to the arrangements for service provision put in place by the authorities. We will review the effectiveness of these arrangements after the first year of operation.

Collection of Commercial Waste

We intend to identify examples of good practice in dealing with the particular problems of commercial waste collection in small towns and villages. This will be published as guidance for the new local councils.

SCOTLAND'S WORKING LANDSCAPE

The Review of Designations

We will review natural heritage designations with a view to simplification and de-regulation consistent with over-arching nature conservation objectives.

Indicative Forestry Strategies

We will review the Indicative Forestry Strategies produced under the 1990 guidance with a view to increasing their usefulness.

"Scotland's Coast"

We will publish a discussion paper on coastal issues which will set out proposals for improving present management, building on the successful approaches already being used in parts of Scotland based on the voluntary principle and partnership working.

Native Woods Management

The Forestry Commission will build on its partnerships within a wider programme to encourage management of native woods, including the establishment of a broadleaved marketing development group to help woodland owners realise the economic potential of their woods.

Community Participation in Forest Management

We will consider how to increase the scope for local community participation in forest management, in the light of research commissioned by the Forestry Commission and taking account of the points raised in the FAPIRA discussion document.

The Scottish House

We wish to see a new standard of rural housing design emerge as a defining symbol for a new and vibrant rural Scotland and have asked for a report on what might be possible. The Enterprise network will consider how best to further encourage the production, use and marketing of traditional materials for new building.

THE CONSULTATIONS

The consultation produced responses from a wide variety of sources, each with its own perspective on the social and economic realities of rural life in Scotland. All the responses, where the respondent permitted it, have been placed in The Scottish Office Library for public examination. This annex records some of the views expressed, without comment or other indication of the Government response to these issues.

The comments noted here are drawn from the written comments received inresponse to approaches to over 900 organisations with an interest in rural Scotland.

- A much more comprehensive and integrated approach towards local health service provision; education; and rural housing strategies was required.

- Those involved in rural representative bodies and in professional or trade associations wanted more to be done to encourage and develop meaningful local involvement in the decision-making process. Rural populations feel remote from centres of power and that their views will be disregarded.

- Environment interests tend to be promoted at the expense of the economic well-being of local communities For example, local populations should have more influence on the designation of SSSIs.

- Not all rural areas are remote: the Central Belt, for example, has a large rural population whose interests cannot be separated from those of Glasgow and Edinburgh.

- The richness and complexity of rural societies, in which social, economic, environmental and demographic factors are all inextricably interlinked and interwoven, will require the development of coherent and comprehensive strategies.

- Local people, businesses and other interests seek a strategic approach to Government policies in rural Scotland.

- More effective use and targeting of existing resources is needed. For this to be achieved, delivery mechanisms must be made more effective and must incorporate an integrated partnership and "bottom-up" approach.

- Rural disadvantage, social exclusion, poverty and the difficulties faced by new small business in rural areas needed to be tackled more vigorously.

- There should be a rural aid fund with priorities established at a Scottish level aimed at both geographical areas and priority client groups. Resources should be delivered through existing mechanisms co-ordinated at the local level by local authorities.

- The lack of a social remit for Scottish Enterprise was perceived as placing lowland Scotland at a disadvantage relative to the Highlands and Islands Enterprise area.

- In provision of such services as health, education, retail networks and local government services, there was a split view on whether people should be taken to services or vice versa. Services should be both locally accessible and of high quality.

- Innovative methods of delivery should be developed and piloted for wider dissemination. Rural demonstration areas offered an approach towards developing and disseminating good practice more generally.

- The development and retention of adequate transportation links of all kinds is regarded as fundamental to the economic and social well-being on rural areas. There was apprehension about the future of rural rail links and the impact of fuel and aviation taxes.

- Better and faster roads may simply accelerate concentration of service provision at the expense of remote and immobile consumers, as well as by-passing established businesses.

- New technology and one-stop shops offer opportunities to reduce the need to travel and schools, post offices, banks and other local facilities could be used as information points.

- Appropriate education and training was vital to encourage economic diversity, and to increase the opportunities available to people in rural areas.

- The land-tenure pattern in the Highlands and Islands was said to have a constraining effect on economic diversity. The landlord-tenant relationship of crofting can inhibit initiatives by crofters.

- Suitable financial incentives and assistance are not available to encourage small-firm development. The Common Agricultural Policy set-aside scheme has reduced the need for support service to agriculture and has resulted in a narrowing of the rural industrial base in such areas as fencing, fertilisers, stock-management.

- In many rural areas, there is limited local added value in agriculture, forestry and fishing production. Significant closures of local sawmills and abattoirs were noted.

- Local enterprise companies are important in securing the marketing, organisational and financial resources which will be required if rural businesses are to develop and diversify, and to take full advantage of the whole economic potential of local products.

- There is potential in tele-working. Technological advances can bring opportunities for relatively highly-skilled employment by enabling professional and skilled clerical functions to be carried out far from urban centres.

- Crofting offers a diverse economic, cultural and environmental base. The use of the land for agricultural production is just one part of the crofting way of life. Restrictions on the use of common land inhibits crofting communities from exploiting economic opportunities and management options.

● Support schemes for crofters are essential and the value of grants should be index-linked. Access to loan capital could provide an alternative to de-crofting of croft houses. A Croft Young Entrants Scheme is required.

● Within Scotland, regional discrimination of the level of CAP direct-income payments is merited on account of the varying conditions in different parts of the country. The Common Agricultural Policy should be reformed away from subsidies on production and towards the provision of integrated support for rural communities.

NOTES

1 Scotland in the Union: A Partnership for Good (1993) HMSO Cm 2225

2 Report of the Committee on Land Utilisation in Rural Areas. (1942) HMSO Cmd 6378

3 House of Lords Select Committee on the European Communities "The Future of Rural Society (1990) HMSO HL Paper 80.

4 The Scottish Office Rural Framework. (1992) The Scottish Office

5 Rural Focus: A Progress Report HMSO 1995

6 Scottish Rural Life: A Socio-economic Profile of Rural Scotland. (1992) The Scottish Office

7 Randall J N. (1985) Scottish Economic Bulletin

8 Advice about setting up community radio stations can be obtained from Mr J Gray, Scottish Association of Small Scale Broadcasters, 13 Comely Bank Row, Edinburgh EH4 1EA.

9 This Common Inheritance (1990) HMSO Cm 1200

10 Council Directive 79/409/EEC on the conservation of wild birds

11 Council Directive 92/43/EEC on the conservation of natural habitats and of wild fauna and flora

12 The Convention on Biological Diversity (1992)

13 Scottish Natural Heritage: Enjoying the Outdoors: A consultation paper on Access to the Countryside for Enjoyment and Understanding. (1994) SNH

14 Cairngorms Partnership, (1994) The Scottish Office

15 Planning Advice Note 32 "Development Opportunities and Local Plans"

16 Planning Advice Notes on "Siting and Design of New Housing in the Countryside" (PAN 36)

"Fitting New Housing Developments into the Landscape" (PAN 44)

Thanks to Scottish Natural Heritage, Historic Scotland, Highlands and Islands Enterprise and the Forestry Commission for the photos used in this document.

Printed in Scotland for HMSO by CC No 13129, Dd 293170, C30, 11/95